THE FEDERAL GOVERNMENT'S ENERGY POLICIES

1978-1979 HIGH SCHOOL DEBATE ANALYSIS

Bittlingmayer, George

American Enterprise Institute for Public Policy Research
Washington, D.C.

0-8447-1829-7
AMERICAN ENTERPRISE INSTITUTE
High School Debate Series
1978

CONTENTS

TABLES

FIGURES

PREFACE

The first two chapters of this book are intended to serve as an introduction to the subject of energy resources and policy in general, and the last three each address one of the 1978–1979 high school debate topics:

Resolved: That the federal government should exclusively control the development and distribution of energy resources in the United States.

Resolved: That the federal government should establish a comprehensive program to significantly reduce energy consumption in the United States.

Resolved: That the federal government should establish a comprehensive program to significantly increase the energy independence of the United States.

The intention has not been to present an extensive and definitive analysis of all the issues raised by the debate resolutions. Rather, the aim has been to provide an introduction to the sources of controversy concerning energy policy. The literature on energy policy is extensive, and no single volume could provide a thorough treatment of the topics with which the well-prepared debater will have to be acquainted. A bibliography has been included to serve as a guide to further research.

Also included in this book is an appendix which contains position statements solicited from the U.S. Department of Energy and various firms and interest groups. Although an attempt was made to obtain a cross-section of informed analysis, these statements should not be considered as representing all possible points of view.

The text for chapters 1, 2, and 4 was prepared by George Bittlingmayer, and that for chapters 3 and 5 by Larry Huckins. Both would like to thank Yale Brozen for his many helpful comments.

Opinions expressed in the analysis are those of the authors and do not necessarily reflect the views of the American Enterprise Institute.

Chapter 1

INTRODUCTION

Whatever other areas of disagreement there may be about energy policy, there is little dispute that modern industrial society can exist only by using large amounts of energy. The scant energy resources that were available to human beings as recently as two or three hundred years ago have been multiplied many times over. Where previously people relied on the strength of their own muscles and the occasional assistance of beasts of burden or wind and water, today a variety of much more powerful and trustworthy ways of getting work done is available. Heat, which our ancestors captured either directly from the sun, to dry agricultural products, for example, or indirectly by burning wood or peat, is now used on a much grander scale and for much more sophisticated purposes.

A moment's reflection on the many ways we use energy underscores its importance to our technology. Energy is needed for more purposes, of course, than heating buildings and fueling automobiles and trucks. While these uses are a large fraction of the total, industrial applications also consume a large percentage of the energy we use each year. The need for energy is obvious in cases like automobile and steel production; but considerable energy also is required to extract minerals such as copper and bauxite, and to produce almost every good imaginable, from glass and paper to transistors and clothing. Even the production of grain products in the United States today requires large amounts of energy for planting, harvesting, and milling.

Reliable sources of energy are necessary for other purposes besides producing goods. A variety of complex devices—computers, medical instruments, and communications equipment, for example—can only be operated if they can depend on reliable power.

Sources of Controversy on Energy Policy

Because energy is central to our way of life, its production and use are controversial and the focus of a great deal of discussion, especially about what governmental policy on the subject should be. A number of issues in particular often motivate and enliven the national discussion about energy policy.

Are Energy Resources Nearly Exhausted? At present the energy we use for so many different purposes comes from only a few sources. Coal, oil, and natural gas, together called fossil fuels, supply roughly 90 percent of the energy consumed each year in the United States. This is remarkable when we consider that fossil fuels have been used on a significant scale for only the last 150 years. Equally noteworthy is the fact that the question of whether and when the earth will run out of coal, oil, and natural gas has been asked almost from the time they were first used.

Where future energy will come from is a proper concern when almost all energy now used comes from sources that are necessarily limited in amount. There is considerable controversy, however, about whether we actually will run out of fossil fuels. Another aspect of the same dispute concerns whether we will run out of cheap energy sources, and if so, whether that is likely to happen soon.

The issue of exhaustible fossil fuel resources is closely linked, of course, to the development of alternative, nonexhaustible sources of power such as solar energy. Obviously, if a practical nonexhaustible power source should be discovered, how much coal and oil remains would become of small concern. However, no such source exists yet—not, at least, at competitive prices.

Estimates vary as to how intensively and for how long we will be able to continue using fossil fuels. Pessimists believe oil and gas may be exhausted as soon as ten or fifteen years from now. We run the risk, it is said, of simply running out of such resources if we continue to use them as fast as we have, and the result could be an industrial collapse.

Most experts, however, think it is a mistake to think in terms of such imminent exhaustion. They contend that we will not, within any relevant time period, run out of fossil fuels, because substantial reserves are still undiscovered. Considerable oil that has been too expensive to bring to the surface so far waits in already discovered wells. As fossil fuel prices gradually rise, this will give oil companies incentives to discover oil in remote areas and to extract more oil from older wells. Rising prices also will induce people to use less of fossil fuels, and at the same time give producers of energy new incentives to develop alternative sources of energy. It is often pointed out that previous predictions that fossil fuels were on the brink of exhaustion, such as were made in the first few decades of this century, did not come true.

At least some of the differences of opinion on this subject can be traced to different estimates of how much oil, coal, and gas are left in the world. Those who are optimistic about the future availability of fossil fuels believe new deposits will continue to be found. Pessimists, on the other hand, believe that most deposits already have been discovered and in large part exploited. The two groups also differ on the question of future technological innovation. If more efficient ways of removing oil from the ground can be developed, for example, we will have much more oil available. Presently only about one-third of the oil in a deposit actually is extracted because of the high cost of extracting the remainder.

Different predictions about the future production and use of energy also result from different conceptions of what governs the actions of business and consumers— that is, how the economy operates. The contrast is most extreme between those who say that the free market cannot be trusted to act in the public interest and those who say that government cannot be trusted to act competently in economic matters. Disagreement on this subject extends to the question of how the use of exhaustible resources can be regulated in the most socially beneficial manner.

The Economy's Response to Changes in Energy Supplies. What would happen if the price of crude oil tripled, or if the amount of available oil fell by half? Would industrial production be crippled, or would we find ways to adjust to such a change without severe effects? The flexibility of the economy and its capacity for adapting to new circumstances are important issues in a discussion of energy policy.

In considering the relationship between our economy and changes in energy supplies and prices, it is important to distinguish between cases in which such changes take place rapidly and cases in which they occur over a long period. The reason for this distinction is that the possibilities for adjustment are greater over long periods than short periods. For the short run, a change in energy supply might mean people will travel less or find ways of traveling that use less energy. Industry might be faced with deciding whether present methods of production could be adapted so as to reduce energy use without prohibitive cost. In the long run, by contrast, a relevant question would be whether it will be possible for industry to develop and install new methods of production that use less energy.

Another question about the flexibility of economic behavior, relevant for both the long and the short run, concerns the interchangeability of different fossil fuels. Is it possible to switch from one fossil fuel to another —oil to coal, for example—as their relative availability changes? Though the answer for the short run may be a qualified yes, major changes of this type are more likely over longer periods.

In addition to more efficient and flexible use of fossil fuels, other responses to changes in the energy situation will be possible and probably necessary. Developing other sources of power, such as nuclear and solar energy, may be one way of combating the higher prices and increased scarcity of oil and gas. Theoretically at least, there are a number of potential alternative sources besides nuclear and solar energy: using temperature differences in ocean waters, tapping the energy in the layers of hot rock beneath the earth's crust, and harnessing the power of the tides are some of the possibilities. However, none of these alternatives has yet proved economical on a large scale.

The question regarding such new sources of energy is, of course, whether their present technological limitations and high costs can be overcome with a reasonable amount of research and development effort. Related to this is the issue of who should do such research and development. Should the government itself launch such programs, or does industry have sufficient incentives and expertise to carry out research and development projects more efficiently?

U.S. Energy Imports. Two circumstances have focused attention on the U.S. practice of importing large proportions of the fossil fuel it consumes. One is the increasing share of yearly energy needs that we import—chiefly from Canada, Venezuela, Nigeria, and Middle Eastern countries. In the period just following World War II, imports of petroleum accounted for only 8 percent of the total petroleum consumed in the United States. By 1967 this figure reached 20 percent, and by 1976 it had climbed to 42 percent.[1]

The second factor that has made the importation of oil a matter of concern to policy makers is the emergence in 1973 of OPEC (the Organization of Petroleum Exporting Countries) as an effective oil cartel. As a result of OPEC actions, the price of oil traded on world markets is much higher than it was before the cartel formed. From 1960 to 1971, the price of oil imported into the United States was less than $4 per barrel. In

1974, the first full year following the beginning of OPEC restrictions, imported oil cost more than $12 per barrel, and by 1976 this figure was up to $14.[2]

High prices are not the only reason why OPEC policies are an important topic in the energy debate. There is also a fear in many Western nations that OPEC countries may again use oil as a political weapon, as some did following the 1973 Arab-Israeli War; that is, they might cut off or threaten to cut off oil supplies in order to win political concessions. A reliable supply of oil is considered essential to the effectiveness of NATO (North Atlantic Treaty Organization) as a military defense, for example, and the European members of NATO obtain most of their oil from the Middle East. There is also a fear that such an oil embargo by some or all of the OPEC states would severely disrupt the economies of countries in Western Europe, which would have damaging consequences for U.S. trade.

Another common question is: What should the United States do about the high price of oil? Should the government impose taxes on imported oil, making the price even higher? Would such a course of action discourage imports and encourage the development of domestic energy supplies? Some experts believe that, acting either alone or in combination with other countries, the United States could counteract the policies of OPEC with such a measure and also reduce its dependence on foreign oil.

Many of those who analyze the problem also argue that the United States' huge oil imports are responsible for the nation's excess of imports over exports as a whole. Further, the decline of the dollar in relation to other currencies is sometimes blamed on the large amount of oil we import. Taxes on imported oil, energy conservation, and increased domestic oil production are often proposed as remedies for correcting both trade deficits and the decline in the value of the dollar.

Energy, Health, and the Environment. The use of almost any type of energy raises questions about possible changes to the environment and effects on people's health and material well-being. Even hydropower can cause environmental damage, such as river silting, and may disrupt and endanger rare vulnerable animal and plant life. Oil, coal, and nuclear power in particular have generated heated controversy about actual and potential environmental damage.

In the case of oil and coal, their extraction from the earth as well as their use can cause pollution. When oil is brought up from off-shore wells, oil spills can occur. Furthermore, regardless of where it is extracted, oil often must be transported over water, which sometimes also results in oil spills. Coal can be mined in two ways, each of which has certain potential dangers. Coal mining underground is hazardous and has been linked with certain occupational diseases, such as black lung. Strip mining, a process by which layers of the earth's crust are removed to allow access to coal, can disfigure the landscape and cause soil erosion if the land is not restored afterwards.

Fossil fuels also affect air quality when they are burned to create energy. Besides being unpleasant, such air pollution is harmful in varying degrees to human health and the environment. Sulphur emissions from auto exhaust, for example, accelerate the deterioration of buildings, and air pollution in general is associated with certain respiratory and circulatory ailments. Natural gas, usually considered to be the cleanest fossil fuel, emits carbon dioxide (as do coal and oil), which some believe has effects on the upper atmosphere.

Nuclear power poses potential problems both of plant safety and of health hazards posed by nuclear wastes. The exact nature and extent of these dangers has not been resolved. Some experts point out that the use of nuclear energy so far has proven to be no more dangerous than the use of coal. Others note that if any accident should happen, it could be a major catastrophe that could cause numerous deaths and long-lasting environmental contamination.

Competition in the Energy Industries. Another source of controversy in energy policy is the common charge that the various firms that supply energy are not competitive. The results, it is said, are a misallocation of resources and prices that are higher than they should be. If firms are not competitive, but instead collude with one another, they can restrict the amount of energy available to consumers and charge considerably more for each barrel of oil than that oil cost to produce.

Various evidence is cited in support of this charge. It is pointed out, for example, that almost 50 percent of the crude oil produced in 1970 came from the eight largest firms. Another occasional charge is that the major oil firms colluded with OPEC in raising the price of internationally traded oil. Also mentioned is the tendency of oil firms in recent years to extend their operations to other energy areas, such as coal mining. The feature of the oil industry that has lately attracted the most public scrutiny, however, is the tendency of the larger firms to integrate vertically. Vertical integration refers to a company's extending the range of its operations through all phases of oil production, from extraction through transportation and refining to marketing the final product.

Those who defend the oil industry point out that many major industries that are generally considered competitive have fewer major producers than oil does. They also argue that vertical integration occurs in many industries, and that it is a natural consequence of the desire of businesses to lower costs, which ultimately results in lower prices to consumers. The difficulties involved in obtaining long-term contracts for crude oil, it is claimed, have induced many oil firms to assure themselves of secure supplies by integrating vertically.

The Effectiveness of Government Energy Policies. A long-standing bone of contention in politics is the charge that government activity in certain areas tends to have more costs than benefits. In the energy field, for example, some observers feel that government regulation, instead of helping consumers over the 1973–1974 energy shortage, contributed to it. The political process, they say, is ill-suited to the close regulation of what is fundamentally an economic concern.

Another area in which government action is said by some to have done more harm than good is the regulation of natural gas prices. By establishing a maximum price for natural gas that was below what suppliers could successfully have charged without regulation, the accusation goes, the government encouraged consumers to use gas wastefully and discouraged its production. Although regulation was originally approved on the ground that gas production was not a competitive activity, the reason government regulation continued, it is said, was political pressure brought to bear by those who were assured of gas at the artificially low price. Others, willing to pay more, could not get gas at any price.

Opponents of this view dispute both the allegation that government policies on gas and other energy issues were generally harmful in the past and the idea that future government energy policies are likely to be counterproductive. They say government activity is needed to ensure that the development, production, and use of energy are carried out in a way that is not socially undesirable. Firms by themselves have no incentive to avoid pollution, and they may be indifferent to the possibility that we will soon run out of fossil fuels. Government policies can ensure that coal and oil production does not take place at too fast a pace, and that consumption is kept at a socially desirable level. Even if unregulated energy production and use worked efficiently, certain income groups or certain regions of the country might bear a disproportionate share of the burdens or benefits, which might call for government intervention. It is sometimes also pointed out that in other industrialized countries, such as Great Britain, the energy industries are under greater government scrutiny and control than they are here.

Those skeptical of government activity generally respond that firms are induced by economic incentives to look for future energy supplies. Because current governmental policies in the United States are designed to provide "cheap energy" by controlling prices, their effect is to create shortages or, if not shortages, then a too rapid exploitation of fossil fuels. If one is worried about the effects that increases in energy prices have on poor people, a more efficient way of helping them would be to provide them with higher incomes that they could spend as they saw fit.

Needless to say, the effectiveness of government in dealing with energy issues is a topic that touches almost every aspect of the energy question. It is the cause for much debate, within as well as outside government. It is therefore of some interest to consider the opinions that political leaders express on energy issues and how they incorporate various energy concerns in their formally stated aims. One such policy statement is the "National Needs Statement" that appeared in President Carter's 1979 budget. The aims set out there are:

- Reduce dependence on foreign oil in the near term and minimize the potential effects of supply disruptions.

- Prepare the U.S. economy to withstand the effects of higher energy prices resulting from continuing growth in demand coupled with the declining availability of world oil supplies.

- Develop renewable and essentially inexhaustible sources of energy for sustained economic growth through the next century.

- Protect the environment while achieving the nation's energy goals.

- Assure that energy policies and programs are fair, equitable, and fiscally sound.[3]

These aims are carefully worded and reflect the necessity in politics of finding areas of agreement. Much has been left unsaid, for very often even where agreement exists on aims, little agreement exists on methods. We shall turn to these methods, but only after a closer look at some of the nuts and bolts of energy use and production.

An Overview of Energy in the United States

In considering the possible future role of the federal government in controlling the production and use of energy, it is important to have some familiarity with the history of energy use in the United States, and to be aware of the factors that are likely to be important in the future. How have our sources of energy changed over time? What are the different uses to which energy has been put? What have the prices of coal, oil, and other fuels been? How are the production and distribution of various types of energy organized?

It is useful in looking at some of the important issues to lump together the various sources of energy, such as coal, oil, and natural gas. Although a ton of coal and a barrel of oil cannot be compared directly, each can be represented by the amount of heat that can be derived from it. One frequently used measure of heat is the Btu (British thermal unit), defined as the amount of heat required to raise the temperature of one pound of water one degree Fahrenheit. A 42-gallon barrel of oil, for example, has about 5.8 million Btu and a ton of coal 25 million.[4] Knowing that and the prices of a barrel of oil and a ton of coal allows us to calculate, for instance, whether heat from one source or the other is cheaper. Often the quantities involved in such calculations are very large. It is convenient in such instances to speak of quadrillions of Btu, a quadrillion being 1,000,000,000,000,000 and represented in scientific notation as 10^{15}. It probably comes as no surprise, but in the jargon of energy experts "quadrillion" is, as often as not, reduced to just "quads."

Domestic Energy Sources. The amount of energy used in the United States in 1947 and 1976, and the sources it came from, are displayed in table 1-1. Energy consumption for 1947 is estimated to have been 33

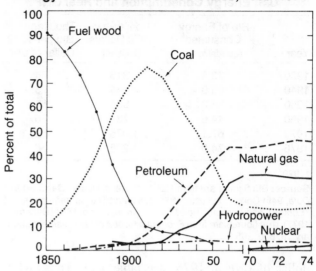

Figure 1-1

Energy Sources in the United States, 1850–1974

Source: U.S., Congress, House, Committee on Interstate and Foreign Commerce, *Basic Energy Data,* 94th Cong., 1st sess., 1975, p. 87.

quadrillion Btu, a quantity which by 1976 had risen to 74 quadrillion Btu. The most important long-run trend in energy sources is the increase in the use of natural gas and petroleum. In 1947 natural gas provided 13.6 percent of the total; by 1976 this had risen to 27.4 percent. Petroleum's share over the same period rose from 44.5 percent to 47.3 percent, while the contribution of hydropower rose only slightly in percentage terms, from 4.0 to 4.1. The new element in energy is of course nuclear power, which by 1976 supplied only 2.7 percent of the total.

One point to keep in mind about energy consumption is that the sources of energy have changed considerably over the last century. Three trends in particular deserve attention (see figure 1-1). First, in 1850, wood was the major source of energy in the United States, supplying 91 percent of the total consumed. It became gradually less important, and by 1950 it supplied only 3 percent. Second, coal-supplied energy provided its greatest fraction of the total—77 percent—in 1910. Its relative importance has declined since then, until only 19 percent of the total was supplied by coal in 1970. Finally, petroleum and natural gas have grown in importance; together they supplied 77 percent in 1970, as large a proportion of the total energy consumed as coal at its peak.

A second statistic that may shed some light on energy use in the United States is the ratio of Btu to real gross national product (GNP).[5] Perhaps surprisingly, this ratio of energy to production has dropped since 1940, going from 73,000 Btu per dollar of GNP to 58,000 Btu per

Table 1-1
Major Sources of U.S. Energy, 1947 and 1976

	1947	1976
Total energy used	33 quadrillion Btu	74 quadrillion Btu
Percent provided by:		
Coal	47.9	18.5
Petroleum	34.5	47.3
Natural gas	13.6	27.4
Hydropower	4.0	4.1
Nuclear power	0	2.7

Source: The Conference Board, "Energy Consumption," *Road Maps of Industry,* no. 1821 (December 1977).

Table 1-2
U.S. Energy Consumption and Real GNP

Year	Btu of Energy Consumed (quadrillions)	Real GNP in 1972 Dollars (billions)	Thousands of Btu per 1972 Dollar of GNP
1930	23.3	315[a]	74
1940	25.0	344	73
1950	35.2	534	65
1960	44.6	737	60
1970	67.1	1,075	62
1976	74.0	1,275	58

[a]1929.

Source: Btu figures are from U.S., Congress, House, *Basic Energy Data*, 94th Cong., 1st sess., 1975, p. 84, and The Conference Board, "Energy Consumption," *Road Maps of Industry*, no. 1821 (December 1977). GNP figures are from *Economic Report of the President*, January 1978, p. 265.

dollar of GNP in 1976 (see table 1-2). Thus, while energy use has more than doubled in that period, production in real terms has risen by an even larger factor. Two sources of this downward trend were increased efficiency in electricity generation and increased efficency of railroad freight transportation resulting from the substitution of diesel engines for steam locomotives.[6] Between 1965 and 1970, however, the ratio of energy consumption to GNP rose: "From the Btu used per dollar of real GNP in 1965 [56,000], the number rose to 62,000 in 1970. While output for the economy as a whole was growing at 3.1 percent per year, energy consumption grew at 5.0 percent."[7]

Earl Cook has suggested that increased demand for electricity explains much of this reduced efficiency in the use of energy from 1965 to 1970. The thermal efficiency of electricity is about 32 percent, while the thermal efficiencies of the fossil fuel processes that electricity replaces are in the neighborhood of 60 to 90 percent.[8] The turnaround since 1970 has been attributed in part to a move away from heavy manufacturing industries toward less energy-intensive production and service industries.[9]

It is also of some interest to compare the relationship between per capita income and per capita energy consumption for various countries (see figure 1-2). Canada and the United States are clearly unusually intensive in their use of energy, even compared with countries having similarly high per capita incomes.

When considering energy data one quickly stumbles into controversial areas. Some economists, for example, argue that Btu measurements, while of some use, can be misleading when we try to account for energy consumption. In particular, they point out that Btu from different sources have different costs. Because

energy policy is fundamentally concerned with costs —costs of extraction, conservation, and pollution abatement—talking about Btu consumption alone does not give us much insight. Reasons why Btu from various sources are priced differently include production costs and government policies.

It costs the economy more in labor and capital resources to supply a Btu of gasoline than to supply a Btu of heating oil . . . If we are to understand the energy market, we cannot add fuels as if their only physical property was the potential units of heat they can be converted to.[10]

Even if one accepts the Btu approach, other disagreements may arise concerning the interpretation of the figures. No agreement exists as to whether the United States' comparatively high energy consumption indicates that we are wasteful with energy. Some experts argue that Americans are using more than a fair share of energy, even when our higher than average incomes are taken into account. Others counter that our intensive energy use is a rational response for people living in a country where energy prices are relatively low and it is common to travel long distances. As an example of the former position, consider the remarks of David Large in a publication of the Conservation Foundation:

The overall energy efficiency of the U.S. economy in 1970 was about 51 percent, meaning that 49 percent of the 64.6 quadrillion Btu consumed was discarded as waste heat and pollution, doing no useful work and often causing adverse environmental impact. . . . Some of that waste results from fundamental physical restraints upon the efficiency [with] which energy can be converted from one form to another, but much of it results from indifferent mechanical design and our tendency to adopt grossly wasteful ways of doing things and getting about, even when more efficient alternatives exist.[11]

Contrasting with this view that Americans' high energy use results from lack of *attention* to efficiency is Melvin Laird's view that it results from the comparatively low *cost* of using energy in this country:

For products from bubble gum to bombers, how much is demanded by consumers is a function of its cost. It is therefore totally unremarkable that in the United States we have the highest energy use per capita, because we also have the lowest energy costs in the free world. In fact the real price of energy fell continuously for three decades right up to the OPEC price escalation and even today is lower in real terms than it has been earlier in our history.[12]

Figure 1-2
Energy Consumption per Unit of GNP for Various Countries, 1974

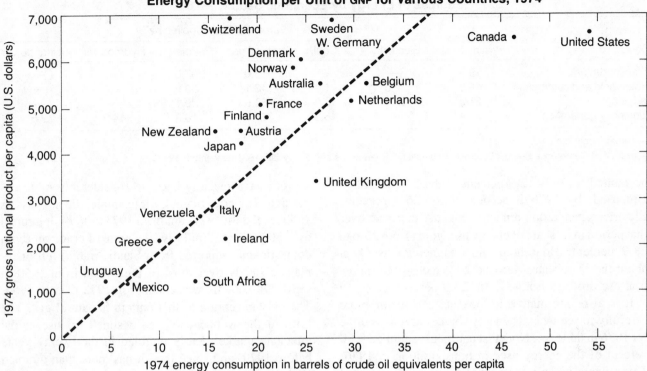

Source: U.S., Executive Office of the President, *The National Energy Plan*, 1977, p. 3.

Energy Imports. Whether expressed in Btu or dollars, the United States imports more energy than it exports, largely in the form of petroleum. Although 42 percent of the petroleum consumed in 1976 was imported, the U.S. "energy deficit," as it is sometimes called, has not always been this large. In 1947, for example, only 8 percent of the petroleum consumed here came from abroad. Most of this increase in oil imports has occurred in the 1970s. As late as 1967 only 20 percent of the oil consumed in the United States came from abroad. But by 1973, the year of the oil embargo, this figure had risen to 36 percent.[13]

Part of the increase in petroleum imports since 1970 can be in part attributed to decreases in domestic production. In 1970, the year of the greatest domestic petroleum production, when 4.12 billion barrels were supplied by producers in the United States, only 1.16 billion barrels, or 22 percent of the total consumed, came from foreign sources. By 1974 domestic production was down to only 3.85 billion barrels, and imports were 2.19 billion barrels, or 36 percent of total consumption.[14] A discussion of the possible reasons for this trend is reserved for later. For the moment, suffice it to say that no agreement exists on the issue. Government price controls and mismanagement, the increasing scarcity of domestic oil, and oil company profiteering have each been blamed.

In other fossil fuel markets, the United States, is close to self-sufficient. In 1974 only 4 percent of the natural gas consumed here came from abroad, mainly from Canada and Mexico. In coal the United States is a net exporter; in 1974 roughly 10 percent of the 596 million tons of coal produced here was shipped abroad.[15]

Energy Uses. The key development since World War II in the way the United States has used energy is the great increase in the percentage of total Btu devoted to transportation (see table 1-3). In 1947 transportation

Table 1-3
Energy Used by Major Economic Sectors, 1947 and 1976

	1947	1976
Total energy used	33 quadrillion Btu	74 quadrillion Btu
Percent used by:		
Transportation	12.9	26.3
Household and commercial	20.5	19.9
Industrial	38.7	24.9
Electricity	26.6	28.9
Miscellaneous	1.3	—

Source: The Conference Board, "Energy Consumption," *Road Maps of Industry,* no. 1821 (December 1977).

Table 1-4
Sources of Energy by Economic Sector, 1976

Sector	Btu Used (quadrillions)	Percent of Btu Supplied by					
		Electricity	Coal	Natural gas	Petroleum	Hydropower	Nuclear power
Transportation	19.3	—	—	3.0	97.0	—	—
Household and commercial	18.8	22.0	1.3	43.1	33.6	—	—
Industrial	21.2	13.4	18.0	39.5	29.1	—	—
Electricity generation	21.4	—	45.3	14.7	16.3	14.2	9.6

— Zero or negligible.

Source: The Conference Board, "Energy Consumption," *Road Maps of Industry,* no. 1821 (December 1977).

accounted for only 12.9 percent of the 33 quadrillion Btu used; by 1976 it accounted for 26.3 percent. Electricity generation remained roughly the same over that period in its share of energy use, going from 26.6 to 28.9 percent. Household and commercial use kept about the same share—around 20 percent—but industrial use dropped from 39.7 to 24.9 percent.

It is also informative to look at each sector more carefully to see what its energy sources are, as is done for 1976 in table 1-4. Note that petroleum supplied 97.0 percent of the energy used in transportation in 1976. This reliance on only one type of energy is not repeated in the other three sectors and reflects certain technical facts of life. Houses, for example, can be heated with oil, natural gas, or coal. They also can be heated with electricity, which is derived in turn from one of those three sources or from hydropower or nuclear sources. Similarly, industrial processes often can be switched with relative ease from using coal to using some oil derivative. At present, however, there seems to be no substitute for gasoline and diesel fuel as a source of inexpensive and convenient power for most transportation uses.

When any type of energy is used, substantial amounts of it are lost. It is sometimes asserted that half the energy used in the United States is used inefficiently. According to estimates made by the Department of the Interior, of the 72 quadrillion Btu consumed in 1972, only 36 quadrillion were efficiently used.[16] Not all this energy loss results from wastefulness: to a certain extent, these figures are measures of technical and not economic efficiency. Suppose, for instance, that it takes less coal to heat a house directly than to generate enough electricity to heat the house to the same temperature. It might nevertheless be not only more convenient, but cheaper as well, to use the coal indirectly.

Energy Prices. A glance at table 1-5, which presents the cost of various energy sources, reveals that all these

sources have recently become considerably more expensive. The price of coal, for example, did not pass its 1950 level until 1971, but from 1973 to 1974, it jumped over 50 percent. Similarly, the price of crude oil (both domestic and imported from Saudi Arabia) fell or remained steady over most of the period from 1950 to 1970. Oil actually was cheaper in 1972 than in 1960. The only exception to this pattern is natural gas. The price at the wellhead of gas destined for use in the interstate market nearly doubled in the twenty years before 1970, and since then it has more than doubled again.

Although some controversy surrounds the interpretation of these figures, it may help to structure further discussion if we briefly outline here the most widely accepted reasons for the patterns seen in table 1-5. First, one should keep in mind that these fuels are to varying degrees substitutes for one another. It is usually technically possible to use two or more fuels for a given purpose—houses, for instance, can be heated with coal, oil, or gas. Furthermore, each fuel has a number of uses. From the standpoint of economics, this interchangeability means that if the price of one fuel goes up because a tax has been imposed or producers (whether OPEC or the oil companies) restrict output, the prices of the other fuels will go up as well, although how far is difficult to establish in advance.

To return to the increases in fuel prices shown in table 1-5, one case where there is no question why prices shot up is that of Saudi Arabian crude oil. The fourfold jump in crude oil prices between 1972 and 1974 resulted directly from the price-setting policies of OPEC, of which Saudi Arabia is the dominant member.

American domestic crude oil prices also have been controlled by price regulations since 1971, although with the aim of keeping prices down rather than up. (An additional rationale for that policy has been that it keeps American producers from making "windfall" gains on their present holdings of oil for which they expected to receive a lower price when they originally developed

Table 1-5
Producers' Prices for Major Energy Fuels
(in 1976 dollars)

Year	Coal (dollars per short ton at mine mouth)	Natural Gas (cents per thousand cubic feet at wellhead)[a]	Domestic Crude Oil (dollars per barrel at wellhead)[b]	Saudi Arabian Crude Oil (dollars per barrel)
1950	10.83	14.5	5.62	NA
1955	9.40	21.7	5.77	NA
1960	9.04	27.0	5.55	2.95
1965	8.41	29.5	5.42	2.52
1970	10.36	28.3	5.26	2.10
1971	11.35	29.2	5.44	2.66
1972	11.77	28.6	5.21	2.83
1973	11.60	29.3	5.29	3.95
1974	18.00	34.7	7.85	12.31
1975	20.13	46.5	8.02	11.21
1976	20.00	58.0	8.18	11.51

NA: Not available.

[a] Interstate controlled price.

[b] Since 1971, average of "old" and "new" controlled prices.

Source: Milton Russell, "Energy," in *Setting National Priorities: The 1978 Budget,* ed. Joseph A. Pechman (Washington, D.C.: Brookings Institution, 1977), p. 319.

them.) However, some authorities on the subject claim that the price controls on domestically produced oil and gas are the reason imports have increased, since price controls restrict the amount of oil producers willingly bring to market. Others contend that the increased imports are due to the declining availability of domestic oil.

Interstate natural gas prices, which were controlled with varying stringency by the Federal Power Commission (FPC) beginning in 1954, have since the mid-1960s been raised at more or less regular intervals. The intrastate gas market, by contrast, is uncontrolled, and prices there have been consistently higher than those shown in table 1-5. The reasons for controlling the price of natural gas need not detain us now, but there are a number of possible reasons why the FPC has found it necessary to raise prices from time to time. The increase in gas pipeline mileage has meant that gas has become available to a larger number of potential customers; at the same time, new environmental regulations have increased the demand for this relatively clean-burning fuel; and the low controlled price itself has increased demand. With the regulated interstate price substantially below the unregulated local price, gas producers have significant incentives to keep gas within the states in which it is drilled.

Coal is perhaps the only fuel currently produced and marketed under conditions close to the free-market ideal. Its price has roughly paralleled the price of oil over time, largely as a result of the ease with which the two can be substituted for each other in electricity generation.

In a more detailed look at how these various energy sources are produced and used, we will again take up the topic of what determines how much coal, oil, and gas we use in the United States, and what determines how much each costs.

NOTES

[1] The Conference Board, "Energy Supply," *Road Maps of Industry,* no. 1820 (December 1977).

[2] Ibid.

[3] U.S., Executive Office of the President, *The Budget of the United States Government, Fiscal Year 1979* (Washington, D.C., 1978), p. 99.

[4] Ford Foundation Energy Policy Project, *Exploring Energy Choices* (Washington, D.C., 1974), p. 1. Btu conversion factors for common fuels are as follows:

1 42-gallon barrel of oil=5.8 million Btu

1 cubic foot of natural gas=1,031 Btu
1 kilowatt hour of electricity=3,413 Btu
1 ton of coal=25 million Btu

[5] Gross national product is the amount of goods and services produced in a country in a given year. *Real* GNP is used when one is concerned with the amount of actual production in terms of machinery, agricultural products, and so on. It corrects for the fact that the prices of most items have gone up over the last forty years. The justification for this is that these things are not really more expensive if, as has been the case, wages and salaries also rise at least as fast.

[6] Richard J. Gonzales, "Future United States Population, Economic Growth, and Energy Demands," *Balancing the Supply and Demand for Energy in the United States* (Denver: University of Denver, Rocky Mountain Petroleum Institute, 1972), p. 6.

[7] *Economic Report of the President,* January 1978, p. 119. The numbers in this quotation have been revised to conform to those in table 1-2.

[8] U.S., Congress, Senate, Committee on Interior and Insular Affairs, *National Goals Symposium: Hearings on Energy and National Goals,* Part II, 92nd Cong., 2nd sess., October 20, 1971, p. 96.

[9] The Conference Board, "Energy Consumption," *Road Maps of Industry,* no. 1821 (December 1977).

[10] Edward J. Mitchell, *U.S. Energy Policy: A Primer* (Washington, D.C.: American Enterprise Institute, 1974), p. 77.

[11] David B. Large, *Hidden Waste: Potentials for Energy Conservation* (Washington, D.C.: The Conservation Foundation, 1973), p. 104.

[12] Melvin R. Laird, *Energy—A Crisis in Public Policy* (Washington, D.C.: American Enterprise Institute, 1977), p. 3.

[13] Conference Board, "Energy Supply."

[14] U.S., Congress, House, Committee on Interstate and Foreign Commerce, *Basic Energy Data,* 94th Cong., 1st sess., 1975, p. 130.

[15] Ibid., pp. 87, 158.

[16] Ibid., p. 112.

Chapter 2

UNITED STATES ENERGY: SOURCES, USES, AND POLICY

Although it can hardly be stressed too much that different energy sources are economically related, in gaining familiarity with energy policy issues it helps to focus on the different sources of energy one at a time. The purpose of such a treatment is to emphasize certain characteristics of American technology and institutions which have shaped past energy policies and probably will continue to do so in the future.

Oil

Regardless of any changes in national policy, the single most important source of energy for the United States over the next decade will be oil. This much is generally accepted in most discussions of the energy problem, which is not to say that it simplifies matters. The present dominance of oil means that its importation, production, and use involve rather large amounts of money, not only for producers and consumers of oil products, but also for producers and consumers of other energy sources. Thus, the incentives are large enough on either side of a number of issues—price controls, oil imports, breaking up the oil companies—to create political complexities that seem to make any happy solution impossible. First we will focus on the basic facts of oil production and use, then on the monumentally bewildering aspects of national oil policy.

Oil Use. Although crude oil can be burned just the way it comes from the ground, it is more economical to refine it into a number of products, each suited to particular uses. In the United States, more crude oil is made into gasoline than any other refined product; in 1973, for example, gasoline accounted for 39 percent by volume of domestic oil consumption.[1] In the same year, distillate fuel oil, which is used primarily for home heating, accounted for 18 percent; residual fuel oil, which is used by electric power plants, industry, and larger commercial and residential buildings, represented 16 percent; and jet fuel constituted 6 percent.[2] The remaining crude oil used by the United States served as the raw material for such products as liquefied gases (propane, for example), kerosene, lubricating

Table 2-1
Petroleum Consumption in the United States by Economic Sector, 1973

Sector	Petroleum Consumed	
	Millions of barrels	Percent of total
Transportation	3,347	53
Household and commercial	1,233	20
Industrial	1,120	18
Electrical generation	557	9
Total	6,298	100

Source: U.S., Congress, House, Committee on Interstate and Foreign Commerce, *Basic Energy Data,* 94th Cong., 1st sess., 1975, p. 137.

oils, asphalt, and coke. A significant amount also is used as feedstock by petrochemical plants that produce such items as plastics, synthetic rubber, fertilizers, and insecticides.

Another way of looking at oil consumption is in terms of the sectors of the economy that use oil products. As table 2-1 shows, in 1973 the transportation sector used more than half of all oil consumed, with most of the rest split among the industrial, household, and commercial sectors. Electric utilities accounted for a small share of the total.

Oil competes directly with natural gas in the home heating market and with coal and natural gas as a boiler fuel in the commercial, industrial, and electric utility markets. Any of these fuels—oil, natural gas, or coal—can be used to provide heat for buildings, to produce steam for industrial purposes, or to generate electricity. But in more than half its markets, oil has no close substitutes. As the energy source for transportation, which accounts for 53 percent of total oil use, oil has no widely practical substitute. The same is true for its use as a petrochemical feedstock, which in 1965 accounted for only 1.7 percent of U.S. petroleum consumption, but by 1976 had nearly doubled to 3.2 percent.[3]

Transportation. While the percentage of oil used by the transportation sector has remained relatively constant, the absolute amount has grown considerably. In 1960 transportation uses accounted for 1,934 million barrels of petroleum; by 1975 those uses absorbed 3,334 million barrels.[4] In trying to account for such an increase, one factor to consider is the number of vehicles in use. Between 1960 and 1975 the number of automobiles increased by 74 percent and the number of trucks by 118 percent.[5] One should, however, avoid concluding that the rise in automobile use "caused" the rise in oil consumption. Aside from the increase in the number of vehicles (which is likely to be related to rises in real gross national product and to the growing size of the adult population), another factor that may help to explain the increase in transportation use of petroleum is the price of petroleum products. Somewhat surprisingly, the price of gasoline (corrected for inflation) fell for most of the post-World War II period; that is, the posted price of gasoline rose less rapidly than prices on the average. Expressed in 1976 dollars, the price of a gallon of gasoline (including tax) went from 63.3 cents in 1950 to a low of 49.2 cents in 1972. This decline was more or less continuous. By 1976 the price had risen to 59.5 cents per gallon, which was still *below* the 1950 price in terms of 1976 dollars.[6]

Households and commerce. In the household and commercial sectors, oil is used primarily for space heating. Although coal was the main competitor in this use years ago, today natural gas and electricity are the major alternatives. Which energy source to use in a given situation depends on price, availability, cleanliness, and convenience. Oil's advantages as a source of space heating are that in many areas it is less expensive than electric heat and easier to obtain than natural gas. Coal, which is inconvenient to use, especially in single-family homes, also has been prohibited in some areas for household use because of environmental and public health concerns.

Industrial consumption. Oil consumption by industry accounts for 18 percent of total domestic consumption of petroleum. Industry differs from the other sectors, however, in that a significant part of the petroleum it consumes is used not as a fuel but as a raw material. In industry the demand for oil as a raw material has increased much more rapidly in the past quarter of a century than has demand for oil as a fuel. In 1947 about 16 percent of industry's total consumption of oil was for nonfuel purposes. By 1972, this proportion had increased to almost 40 percent. Much of industry's nonfuel petroleum goes for use as petrochemical feedstock. The remainder is used to produce wax, lubricants, asphalt, and assorted other products.

Government policies affecting oil use. A number of government policies influence the amount of oil Americans use and the ways we use it.

1. Excise taxes: Several different federal excise taxes relate to oil consumption either directly, such as the manufacturer's excise tax on gasoline, or indirectly, such as the use tax on highway vehicles. All these taxes tend to reduce the consumption of petroleum, some by raising fuel prices, others by raising the cost of vehicles.

2. Oil import restrictions: From 1959 until 1973 the United States had a system of import controls (quotas) which limited the amount of oil that could be brought into this country from abroad. In 1973 this system was altered, and a small "fee" (tax) on imports above the old quota levels was imposed. Both the quota and the fee system have had several effects. By tending to reduce the supply of oil available to domestic consumers, they have tended to raise oil prices, thereby stimulating exploration for domestic oil sources (in the absence of domestic price controls on oil). While the quota was in effect, world prices for crude oil were lower than U.S. prices. The quota kept foreign oil from displacing domestic oil, however, and encouraged domestic exploration beyond what otherwise would have occurred. The effect economists predicted for the new fee system—an increase in oil imports (but still to less than free-trade levels)—has been enhanced somewhat by price controls on domestic oil, which discourage domestic production and, some claim, also induce producers to hold oil off the market if they expect that the controls may be lifted. By keeping American oil at a price lower than that of world oil, this policy has served to lower the *average* price Americans pay for crude oil, at the expense of increased imports.

3. Subsidies to automobiles: Some observers feel that state and local governments heavily subsidize automobile transportation by not charging drivers the full cost of providing services for their automobiles. Parking meters may cost 10 cents an hour, for example, while the market rate is reflected in the price of 75 cents an hour charged by parking lots. Automobiles impose both financial and personal burdens on the rest of society with their noise and air pollution, yet drivers are not taxed to correct for these impositions. The cost of traffic control and road construction is borne by all the citizens of a city, even though automobile drivers benefit most from these expenditures. The list could be extended. According to this line of argument, all these subsidies make it cheaper to drive a car than if automobiles paid their own way, and thus they stimulate the demand for gasoline.

Production. Finding oil is a complicated process. First oil explorers narrow the range of possible well locations, using various techniques that rely on small changes in gravitation, the way shock waves from explosions are transmitted through the earth's crust, and geological mappings. Firms looking for oil must obtain a lease fairly early in their explorations from the owner of the property where they are searching. The lease is granted by the owner if the land is private property and by the federal government if it is public. Leases allow firms to conduct their investigations on the land, and they stipulate how much the owner gets in royalty payments if oil is found.

Even if, on the basis of the evidence it has gathered, a firm decides to drill on the land, there is only about one chance in ten that oil will be found. Furthermore, if oil is obtained from a well, more drilling has to be done to determine the extent of the oil reservoir. Some pools are simply not put into production because they contain too little oil.

The means usually used to bring oil to the surface is called "natural drive." Crude oil is located in porous rock and is under pressure, either from surrounding water or from natural gas deposits, which often lodge with the oil. During the initial stages of extraction, the pressures exerted by the water and any gas deposits are enough to bring the oil to the surface. At later stages, when this "natural drive" exhausts itself, oil crews can bring more oil to the surface by fracturing the rock with explosives and by pumping up the oil. Even with such methods, usually only between 20 and 40 percent of the oil in a reservoir is recovered. For fields discovered between 1935 and 1969, the cumulative recovery efficiency (the proportion of oil recovered) was 30.3 percent.[7]

But what happens if an oil pool extends beyond a property's boundaries? Before the 1930s holders of mineral rights were permitted to take as much oil as they could by drilling on their property, whether or not they drew oil from under other properties. This led to competitive drilling, with each party attempting to extract as much of the common pool as possible at the expense of other nearby property owners. Not surprisingly, the result was extremely rapid exploitation of oil fields, which is generally agreed to be undesirable.

A number of solutions are possible to prevent overly rapid exploitation. Those drilling could agree to merge and operate the field as one unit; the problem with this idea is that the owners often disagree on how each one's share should be determined and enforced. Another solution might be the same sort of "unitization" enforced by the state. During the 1930s the solution in a number of oil-producing states was for the state governments to allocate a share of the production to each of the land-owners. The rate of extraction was called the "maximum efficient rate of production" or MER. Along with this, a statewide restriction on production was often imposed. These two measures were implemented in a number of states, including major oil producers such as Texas, Oklahoma, and Louisiana, and together they came to be called "market-demand prorationing."

The rationale for the MER regulation has been set out by William J. Murray, Jr., a former chairman of the Texas Railroad Commission, one of the state agencies that enforced market-demand prorationing.

Without proration by a state regulating authority, each producer is legally entitled to all the oil he can capture and sell from a common oil reservoir. There are no fences underground. It is always open range and the law of capture applies as far as the oil man is concerned. Without proration a wasteful flood of oil would recur as in the early life of the East Texas Field.[8]

Others are not as convinced that the market-demand prorationing system had the efficient production of oil as its only objective. Edward J. Mitchell, professor of business economics at the University of Michigan, sees the system as an attempt to raise prices of crude oil under state direction.

From the 1930s to at least 1970 . . . the U.S. crude oil producing market was not free. It was cartelized. A cartel exists when there are either restrictions on who can sell in a market or on how much anyone can sell. Oil production under market-demand prorationing was cartelized because producers' output was restricted by regulatory commissions.[9]

Mitchell concludes that "the domestic cartel price was substantially above the price that would have existed in a competitive market with unitized fields."[10]

Reserves. Oil experts use various measures in estimating how much petroleum is still in the ground. Very often they speak of "reserves" or "proven reserves," usually referring to already-discovered oil that can be extracted using existing technology and sold at existing prices without economic loss to the producer. Reserves themselves are divided into two categories: measured reserves, and indicated and inferred reserves. To these is sometimes added a third, nonreserve category, undiscovered recoverable resources. This refers to oil that is believed to exist on the basis of geological evidence and which can be extracted without economic loss. The sum of all three categories is called "recoverable petroleum resources."

These different categories are used because determining how much oil there is in a given area is an expensive undertaking, and the expense varies directly with how precise an estimate is desired. Firms that extract oil normally do not attempt to assure themselves of an advance supply of oil beyond ten or twelve years:

Reserves amount to current inventory of minerals in the ground. As mineral production proceeds, material is withdrawn from inventory and reserves are diminished. At the same time, as investments are made in developing additional deposits, new inventory is created and reserves are increased. Current reserves at any given time reflect the interplay of these opposing tendencies. Reserves can be measured in terms of the reserve-to-annual-production ratio, which equals the number of years that the inventory would last if production continued at its present rate and if no new inventory were developed. Economic forces keep the reserve-to-production ratio for many minerals at something like 10–20 years. Larger ratios tend to be uneconomic because the investment required to develop additional reserves would be made too long in advance of any expected return on the additional reserves.[11]

The difficulties involved in using reserve figures, even the more optimistic ones, are illustrated in table 2-2. Notice that the estimate of recoverable oil resources kept growing from 1948 until 1972. If we used the 1948 figure for yearly oil consumption—about 2 billion barrels—a prediction made in that year about how much oil would remain in 1975 (under the assumption that the recoverable resource figure includes all exploitable oil) would have placed 1975 resources at 56 billion barrels. In fact they were 249 billion barrels. Estimates of natural gas resources follow a similar pattern.

When we turn to less optimistic reserve figures, the situation looks even worse. Going by conservative estimates, America has had less than a dozen years' proven supply of oil left for the past hundred years. In 1866 the United States Revenue Commission was concerned about how synthetics could be produced when crude oil production ended; in 1891 the U.S. Geological Survey predicted that there was little chance of finding oil in Texas; and in 1941 the Bureau of Mines estimated total future U.S. production at 6 billion barrels—an amount we have produced every twenty months for years.

Why past predictions have been so far off the mark is explained partly by the fact that reserve figures are arrived at only through a very roundabout method of estimation. There is no way of directly measuring reserves, for the oil is trapped in porous rock as far down as 25,000 feet or more. Any estimate of how much oil there is in a given reservoir comes from the measured flow at the well, from the information further drilling may provide, and from geological information. In other words, the true amount of reserves in even the best of circumstances can only be guessed.[12]

The diagram in figure 2-1 is often suggested as an aid to clear thinking on the subject of oil reserves. The entire rectangle represents all oil still in the ground. Horizontally it is divided between discovered and undiscovered oil. To be properly cautious and to sound properly professional, we can say that, as we move from right to left in the diagram, oil deposits of "increasing degree of geological assurance" are being represented. Similarly, as we move up the side of the diagram, oil deposits are represented that are less and less expensive to extract; that is, they have "increasing economic feasibility." Thus, as figure 2-1 suggests,

Table 2-2
Estimates of Oil and Gas Resources Remaining in the United States

Year of Forecast	Supply of Recoverable Resources	
	Oil (billions of barrels)	Natural gas (trillions of cubic feet)
1948	110	—
1952	—	400
1956	300	856
1965	400	2,000
1969	—	1,859
1970	432	—
1972	458	1,980
1975	249	1,227

— Not estimated.

Source: "Oil and Gas Resources—Welcome to Uncertainty," *Resources* (Washington, D.C.: Resources for the Future, March 1976), p. 2.

Figure 2-1
Estimated United States Crude Oil Resources (1974)
(billions of barrels)

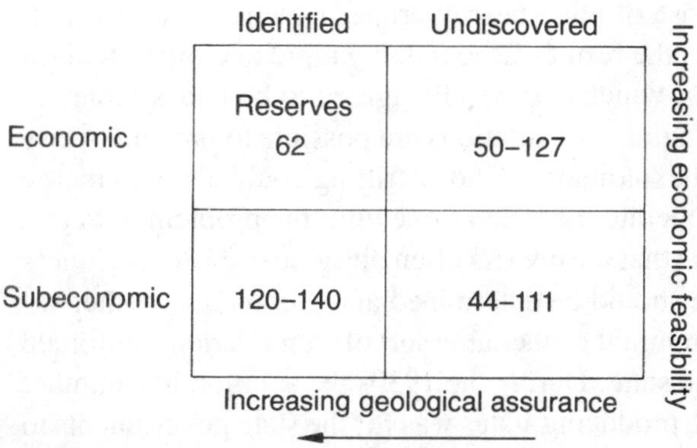

	Identified	Undiscovered
Economic	Reserves 62	50–127
Subeconomic	120–140	44–111

Increasing geological assurance

Increasing economic feasibility

Source: *Resources,* March 1976, Figure 4, p. 8.

one can think of the oil still in the ground as falling into four categories: (1) discovered oil that is worthwhile to extract with current technology and at today's prices, (2) discovered oil that is not worthwhile to extract, (3) undiscovered oil that will be worthwhile to extract, and (4) undiscovered oil that will not be worthwhile to extract.

The United States gets its domestic oil from a number of widely scattered oil fields. These fall generally into three major categories: coterminous onshore, Alaska onshore, and outer continental shelf or offshore. Coterminous onshore petroleum is sometimes called "oil from the lower forty-eight." This refers to the output of wells in Texas, Oklahoma, Louisiana, and a number of other states. According to the U.S. Geological Survey, coterminous onshore petroleum accounts for about 56 percent of the total U.S. recoverable petroleum resources, or between 153 and 276 billion barrels. Alaska onshore petroleum refers to underground reservoirs in Alaska, believed to hold between 40 and 70 billion barrels of recoverable petroleum. Outer continental shelf (OCS) or *offshore* oil comprises underwater fields in the Gulf of Mexico, off the Atlantic and Pacific coasts, and off the north shore of Alaska. Total OCS recoverable petroleum is estimated to be between 75 and 144 billion barrels.

These estimates, which were released in 1974 by the U.S. Geological Survey, show total domestic recoverable petroleum between 273 and 493 billion barrels. A more conservative statistic, based on measured reserves plus indicated and inferred reserves, estimates between 73 and 93 billion barrels.[13] To put these figures in perspective, U.S. petroleum production in 1977 was 3.6 billion barrels, and total consumption was 6.7 billion barrels.

If we shift our focus to the amount of crude oil reserves in the world, one fact immediately becomes obvious: a very large share of that oil is in the Middle East. In 1974 measured world oil reserves were estimated at 542 billion barrels, and Middle East measured reserves constituted 316 billion barrels of that total. The United States, by contrast, had measured reserves of only 35 billion barrels. Although these estimates of measured reserves are the most cautious figures available, they give a fairly accurate idea of the relative shares of oil resources in the world today.[14]

Prices. Generally, speaking about energy prices means in effect speaking about the price of crude oil. Not only is petroleum the largest component of the world's current energy supply, and likely to remain so for some time, but its price strongly influences most other energy prices.

At present, crude oil prices for the United States are not determined in the market, as they are, for example, in the case of coal. Rather, they are set by OPEC and the U.S. government: OPEC determines the price of most oil traded internationally, including imports to the United States, and our government determines the price of domestically produced oil. This has not always been so. As table 1-5 shows, oil prices (when corrected for inflation) were quite stable from 1950 to 1973: domestic prices ranged in the neighborhood of $5 to $6 per barrel, and Saudi Arabian oil between $2 and $3 per barrel (in 1976 prices).

An important fact about the price of crude oil, whether determined by the market or set by cartels or governments, is that changes in that price have not been fully reflected in the prices of refined petroleum products. For example, although the price of imported crude oil rose by 50 percent between 1970 and 1976, and the domestic price by 60 percent, the price of gasoline to the consumer rose by less than 20 percent (in real terms). Over the same period, the price of fuel oil also rose by 50 percent. Meanwhile, the prices of electricity and natural gas, which are both regulated by federal or state agencies, rose by about 10 and 30 percent respectively.[15]

The failure of refined product prices to rise as fast as crude oil prices results from the fact that crude oil prices are only one of several factors contributing to the price of refined oil products. Besides taxes, there are the costs of capital equipment (such as refineries and transportation equipment) and the wages and salaries of oil company employees.

Although the different participants in the energy debate accept the same figures on oil prices, they do not agree on how those figures should be interpreted. Some argue, for example, that in the absence of price controls the oil corporations set prices, that is, they engage in monopolistic practices. Others contend that prices determined without the heavy hand of government would give the true resource value of oil and oil products.

One view about the importance of market prices is expressed by Harvard economist Hendrik Houthakker:

To the economist, the problem of energy, sometimes with much exaggeration called "the energy crisis," is primarily a matter of prices. The question facing us is not, and presumably will not be in the future, whether energy supplies will be sufficient to meet the demand, even though that is the formulation often raised in popular discussions. Unless price controls are going to be a permanent component of our economic institutions—which I neither hope nor expect—supply and demand in energy markets are going to balance at some price.[16]

Oil Policy Issues. Federal government policy has been an important factor in the oil industry since at least 1911, when the Supreme Court upheld a lower court decision ordering Standard Oil to divest itself of its major components. Other policies since then have included special tax provisions for the oil industry, regulation of the exploration and development of public lands, restrictions by state governments on oil production, and price controls. Some policies, such as the application of the Sherman Antitrust Act in the Standard Oil case, are directed at business in general. Others, such as price controls, are aimed only at oil.

Price controls on oil. Discussions about whether oil prices should be influenced by taxes or other controls revolve around three issues: (1) the best ways to promote the efficient use of oil; (2) the distributional effects between producers and consumers and various income groups; and (3) the use of such policies to minimize or counteract any harmful effects resulting from OPEC policies.

In the past, one important factor in the conditions under which oil was produced was the market-demand prorationing scheme described earlier. Most observers agree that that system drove domestic crude oil prices up, although whether they rose higher than economic efficiency demanded is open to dispute.

A second influence, one that tended to increase oil supplies, was the recently curtailed oil depletion allowance. Oil producers were allowed to reduce their taxable income by a certain percentage of the value of the crude oil they produced.

A third major policy measure was the import quota system in effect until 1971. This restricted the amount of cheaper foreign oil coming into the United States and allocated it among producers. The result of limiting such imports was that petroleum product prices were higher than they otherwise would have been.

Throughout the 1950s and '60s, government, through the institutions of market-demand prorationing and import quotas, gave us a surplus policy toward the domestic producing industry. Excess capacity existed in domestic oil production because prices were higher than necessary to clear the market. While this policy gave consumers substantial protection against cutoffs of foreign supplies and insulated the U.S. market from the vagaries of the world market, it also placed heavy costs on U.S.

consumers and wasted billions of dollars in unnecessary drilling activity.[17]

Although market-demand prorationing is still a part of state governments' policies, it is not currently effective in reducing domestic supplies. For most practical purposes, depletion allowances and oil import quotas are no longer in force either. Since the world price of oil increased above the domestic price in 1973, the United States has instituted price controls on domestic oil, and it has set up an "entitlement" program aimed at equalizing costs between producers who use varying percentages of domestic and foreign oil. American oil producers currently pay not two but three different prices for crude oil. Oil imported from OPEC countries is the most expensive. Oil from newly discovered U.S. deposits is controlled at a somewhat lower price; and oil from old oil wells is priced the lowest. Without controls or tariffs, all oil would have the same price, namely one determined by world supply and demand (except for regional differences because of transport costs).

The justification for price control programs generally follow one of three themes. The first is that the oil industry is not competitive, and domestic price controls are necessary to keep oil producers from exploiting the consumer now that OPEC has increased the price of oil on the world market. The second is that an uncontrolled market would result in windfall profits to producers for oil they developed when oil prices were low. The third is that continued price regulation is necessary to shield consumers, and especially lower-income citizens, from higher prices.

The last two concerns can be seen in President Carter's National Energy Plan: "If producers were to receive tomorrow's prices for yesterday's discoveries, there would be an inequitable transfer of income from the American people to the producers, whose profits would be excessive and would bear little relation to actual economic contribution."[18]

Melvin Laird criticizes this approach, however, contending, "The continued price regulations coupled with uncertainty over future policy directions on oil have dampened incentives to find and produce more domestic oil, a result directly contrary to the increasing dependence on foreign oil."[19] Laird suggests that letting prices of crude oil rise to the world level would be the best solution because it would establish proper incentives for consumers to conserve and domestic producers to provide supplies of oil. He suggests that "in the case of 'windfall' profits, from the standpoint of increasing energy supplies the ideal result might be to realize them and have them plowed back into energy exploration and development."[20] In the event that this is politically impossible, such profits could be taxed away with a one-time levy—the main goal is to remove the price controls.

Walter J. Mead, professor of economics at the University of California, Santa Barbara, questions whether it is appropriate at all to talk about "windfall" profits:

For all remaining oil reserves, substantial inventory profits would occur as a result of the large increase in crude oil prices. These profits would be shared by private and government landowners in the form of royalty payments, and lessees consisting of about 10,000 crude oil producers. An increase in inventory value resulting simply from a fortuitous price increase is sometimes referred to, in derogatory spirit, as a "windfall." But "windfall profit" is not an analytic concept, and it is not useful in determining public policy for the following reasons:

1. For all oil discovered on leases purchased after about 1974, when prices reached their present level (adjusted for inflation), the term "windfall gain" would not be appropriate if applied to producing oil companies. It would apply to the royalty interest, but in most cases the royalty interest is owned by federal or state governments.

2. Apart from the politics involved in the windfall gain terminology, it is not clear from the point of view of economic analysis that there are windfall gains even for reserves existing prior to 1973. Oil is a nonrenewable resource. It is possible that owners of oil reserves have long been expecting price increases . . .

3. If the government is to use the windfall gain concept as an excuse for price controls, then why single out crude oil prices when some other prices also have increased sharply? Spot prices of coal and of Douglas fir timber, for example, have both increased fourfold since 1967. Similarly, spot uranium prices (yellow cake) have increased in about the same proportion.

4. How long are prices to be controlled in the name of historical windfall gains? The longer prices are controlled, the greater are the distortions and the greater the accumulated cost of administration, both for the government and for complying industry.[21]

Another view about how to deal with increasing energy imports and the effects of high prices is offered by Carter Henderson, codirector of the Princeton Center for Alternative Futures. He suggests gasoline rationing, presumably in addition to existing controls, as an equitable way of reducing energy imports and reducing energy consumption overall.

Raising the price of domestic oil to world levels by removing controls would result in windfall profits to producers . . . while restricting imports through a presidentially imposed quota-allocation program would invite manipulation by the powerful oil industry for its own financial advantage.

Gasoline rationing can cure our excessive appetite for foreign oil fairly and effectively.[22]

However, rationing is considered by most policy experts to be a cumbersome, inefficient, and unpopular way of restricting imports or dealing fairly with lower-income consumers.

Foreign oil. How much oil we import in the United States depends on the incentives American firms have to produce and distribute oil, and the incentives consumers have to use it. Freeing the price of domestic oil is one method of reducing imports, as it would increase the incentive of American producers. Likewise, placing a tax on oil products would lower consumers' incentive to buy them. Both these tactics rely on changes in price to bring about the specific policy objective of increased energy independence, but they may be politically unpopular. Other methods of controlling imports, such as subsidizing domestic production or funding research to improve efficiency in energy use, are also possible.

As we saw earlier, there is still a considerable supply of oil left in the Middle East which can be extracted profitably under present conditions. In 1973 this area's estimated share of world oil reserves was 58 percent, although it is distributed unevenly among the Middle Eastern countries. Saudi Arabia, Kuwait, Iran, Iraq, and the United Arab Emirates are among the most important suppliers. These are also the countries that dominate OPEC, determine its policies, and enable it to restrict output and raise prices. OPEC's justification for forming was the need members felt to respond "to the unilateral decision of the multinational oil companies to cut posted prices in February 1959 and again in August 1960, thus inflicting severe damage to the economies and development programs of oil producing countries."[23] Its policies have, however, taken on a more sinister slant, at least in the minds of people in non-OPEC countries. Many foreign observers believe the cartelization of the oil-producing nations, and particularly the expressed readiness of some of them to use oil for political purposes, poses a serious threat to the world economy and possibly to world peace.

What can the United States do to reduce prices charged by the oil cartel? At first glance, one might imagine that simply reducing imports would have that effect, but this is not necessarily true. What determines whether a cartel raises or lowers its price is the responsiveness of purchasers to changes in price. That is, if American buyers of foreign oil are willing to purchase the same amount whether the price is low or high, the Arab countries have no incentive to lower it. It is not certain that reducing imports would make remaining oil import demand in the United States any more responsive to price. Therefore, American energy policy vis-à-vis the cartel should focus on making our own import demand more sensitive to price. If higher prices mean a large drop in our oil imports from the producing countries and lower prices mean a large increase, we are more likely to get lower prices than if imports are insensitive to price.

Unfortunately, some present and contemplated policies have the opposite effect. Price controls on domestic oil mean that any increase in the price that oil companies must pay for imported oil is not passed on fully to the consumer. With domestic oil supplying 60 percent of U.S. consumption, an increase of one dollar per barrel in the cartel price means only a forty-cent increase in the price to the American consumer. Price controls, by partially insulating the consumer from the cartel, encourage the cartel to charge him or her a higher price. (Fortunately, most major consuming nations have not adopted this policy.) Furthermore, the lower the domestic price, the smaller domestic supplies will be—and the more high-priced foreign oil we will buy.

The Carter administration has proposed, instead of completely removing the price controls on domestic oil, establishing a crude oil equalization tax. This tax would raise the price of domestic crude oil to the "replacement value"—what it would cost the oil company to find and produce that much oil from new sources—but it would not, according to some critics, stimulate American producers to increase their supply. Another part of the administration's program would develop a billion-barrel reserve by 1985, the purpose being to insulate the United States from supply disruptions.

The oil industry and competition. One of the continuing controversies about the domestic petroleum industry is whether it is better characterized as an oligopoly or a shared monopoly than as a competitive industry. (In a competitive industry, by definition, no firm controls enough of the supply to have more than a negligible effect on the amount of a product offered for sale or the price that product will command.)

The combination of rising prices for petroleum products and falling domestic production stimulated a serious effort in the Congress to force the large oil companies to divest themselves of many of their holdings,

that is, to break up each vertically integrated firm into several smaller firms. The charge, as put by Senator Birch Bayh, is:

The lack of competition in the oil industry is the result of the unique convergence of two features: intense concentration and vertical integration. Neither of these economic phenomena is automatically anti-competitive; however, in concert they provide a small number of companies with extensive control over an essential commodity.

The intensity of the concentration in the oil industry can be demonstrated by an accurate recitation of the industry's vital statistics:

Production—In 1973 the 20 largest oil companies accounted for 76.3 percent of the crude oil production in the United States. Moreover, the Federal Trade Commission has estimated that in 1970 these same 20 companies accounted for 93.5 percent of this nation's reserves of crude oil.

Transportation—In 1973 the 16 largest oil companies controlled pipelines that received 92 percent of the crude oil in all pipelines reporting to the Interstate Commerce Commission.

Refining—Also in 1973, the 20 largest oil companies maintained 82.9 percent of the total U.S. refinery capacity.

Marketing—Once again, using the 1973 figures, those same 20 companies accounted for 77.2 percent of the total U.S. gasoline market.[24]

Bayh's attack focused on concentration—a large amount of control in relatively few hands—and vertical integration—control by one company of more than one phase of the same industry. Another issue is horizontal integration, the increasing tendency of oil companies to undertake operations in energy areas besides oil. This too is seen by some as a practice that could create—or perhaps has created—monopoly power. Former Senator John Tunney makes the following points:

In terms of horizontal concentration, oil companies already own more than 35 percent of the existing coal reserves and five oil companies are among leaseholders who control 70 percent of the recoverable deposits on Federal lands . . .

A classic example of how horizontal expansion by the oil giants can adversely affect the consumer is found in the geothermal fields of California, where the price for this potentially cheap source of energy is, strangely enough, under contract, tied automatically and directly to the prevailing price of oil.[25]

Tunney cites a Federal Trade Commission report that estimates that American consumers pay "as much as $180 billion annually because of economic concentration in industry." Furthermore, charges Tunney, "other economic costs that have been linked under concentration include inflation, recession, unemployment, environmental deterioration, periodic shortages, misallocated capital and other interferences with the operation of the free market."[26]

Critics of the views expressed by Senators Bayh and Tunney make two counterarguments: that the degree of concentration and its costs are greatly exaggerated, and that the attempt to break up the oil companies would take about ten years and be very expensive. M. A. Adelman is among those who believe divestiture would be counterproductive, in the literal sense of the word:

Divestiture would slow down the development of new oil supply. It would force the management of every oil company to push to the back burner its projects for exploration and development, in or out of OPEC nations, as well as its plans for increased recovery from known oil deposits, or the development of nonoil energy sources. The reasons for this distraction and wasted effort are painfully simple. The current value of oil industry fixed assets, revalued into current dollars, is over ten times as great as the investment to be made in any given year. A company ordered to divest most of its assets will serve its stockholders by spending management time on getting the most out of the split-up of existing assets, not on planning for new spending which is only one tenth as large. From the standpoint of society, this is all wasted effort. Investment in old and new energy sources, on the other hand, is valuable in itself.[27]

Other critics of the divestiture effort contend that concentration in a majority of other industries is greater than in oil, and that vertical integration is not an attempt to gain or extend monopoly control but is instead a form of organization that keeps costs low and ensures supplies of oil. In the words of David J. Teece:

Vertical integration in the U.S. petroleum industry is the result of competitive pressures and the inherent nature of the oil business. It is a device to lower costs by overcoming the disabilities that market contracting can experience . . . Allegations of market power from vertical integration have been rejected on both theoretical and empirical grounds. The evidence instead points to an industry that is in fact highly competitive.[28]

Natural Gas

The natural gas industry in the United States comprises companies of three general types: production, pipeline, and distribution. Producers search out and develop natural gas reserves and contract with pipeline companies to whom they deliver gas over some negotiated period. Pipeline companies generally purchase the gas in the field (that is, at the wellhead), transport it to market, and sell it, either to distribution companies for resale or directly to industrial customers. Distribution companies are usually public utilities that sell to residential, commercial, and industrial customers.

Natural Gas Production. Most of the gas produced in the United States comes from Arkansas, Louisiana, Oklahoma, and Texas. In 1971, when total domestic production was 22 trillion cubic feet, 18 trillion came from these four states. In all, about 30,000 companies produce oil and gas, but of these only 3,750 sell gas across state lines. The twenty largest of these interstate producers sold 71 percent of the total gas produced by interstate companies in 1971. The largest, Humble Oil, sold 9.2 percent. These interstate producers are regulated by the Federal Energy Regulatory Commission (FERC), the successor to the old Federal Power Commission.

The interstate pipelines of which there were 103 in 1971, also are regulated by the federal government. The regulation is similar in form to that for most electric utilities and phone companies: rates are set so that costs of operation are covered and stockholders get a return on their investment that is considered fair by the regulatory authorities. Most of the distributors to whom the pipeline companies sell natural gas are regulated in a similar manner.

Natural Gas Reserves. Almost all natural gas consumed in the United States—96 percent in 1974 —comes from domestic sources. Although use of gas grew at a yearly rate of 4.1 percent from 1960 to 1974, the increase has not been uniform over the years. Since 1970, the rate of increase has declined sharply, causing shortages. This change has been the subject of the "natural gas shortage" debate—the question being whether the gas companies, the government, or some combination of the two were responsible for the shortages of gas that have occurred.

More disagreement exists on another subject: How much natural gas is left? According to the U.S. Geological Survey, natural gas resources in the United States are as follows:

Measured resources	266 trillion cubic feet
Indicated and inferred resources	130–150 trillion cubic feet
Undiscovered recoverable reserves	1000–2000 trillion cubic feet
Total	1396–2515 trillion cubic feet[29]

The dispute centers on the last of the three categories, undiscovered recoverable resources. Estimates of this quantity vary from 304 to 2,000 trillion cubic feet.[30] The differences are due largely to different interpretations of the same geological data.

Natural Gas Consumption. The use of natural gas for fuel is largely a phenomenon of the last two decades. Before World War II, when there was no economical way of transporting gas more than moderate distances, markets were confined to the immediate producing area. With the development of economical long-distance pipelines, the large natural gas reserves discovered in the search for oil became available nationwide as fast as pipelines and distribution systems could be constructed. In 1946, 4.9 trillion cubic feet of natural gas were produced in the United States. By 1974 this had more than quadrupled to 22.8 trillion cubic feet.

Natural gas has two basic markets: the residential and commercial market, where it is used for heating homes and offices, cooking, and fueling water heaters; and the industrial and electric utility market, where it is used as a boiler fuel to produce direct heat or steam for industrial processes and electricity generation. In the residential and commercial markets, which accounted for 33 percent of total gas consumption in 1968, gas competes mainly with home heating oil. In the industrial and electric utility markets, which accounted for 64 percent of gas consumption in 1968, it competes with coal and heavy fuel oil (as well as hydropower and nuclear energy in the electric utility sector). The remaining 3 percent of natural gas is used in the transportation sector.

A principal factor behind the demand for gas during the 1960s was its low price. The price of natural gas, when sold at the wellhead for interstate delivery, was at that time controlled by the Federal Power Commission (now the Federal Energy Regulatory Commission). Many observers have concluded that the regulated price was and is lower than what would be charged if there were no regulation. One estimate is that the price of a thousand cubic feet of gas would have averaged about 6 cents more during 1961–1968 if there had been no control of wellhead prices.[31]

Price regulation and its effect on demand also have influenced the geographical distribution of gas consumption. Since federal regulations apply only to gas sold to interstate pipelines, intrastate pipelines have been able to buy up most of the newly produced natural gas simply by offering a higher price than the interstate lines are allowed to pay. In 1966, 83.7 percent of newly produced natural gas was sold in the interstate market; by the first half of 1970, the relative positions of interstate and intrastate lines had more than reversed, and only 9.1 percent of newly produced gas went to interstate markets (see table 2-3).

Improvements in pipelines also have stimulated the consumption of gas. In the early 1950s there were abundant reserves of natural gas but few pipelines, which naturally tended to depress gas prices. During this period, prices were incorporated into long-term (ten–twenty year) contracts between the pipeline companies and the gas producers. As the pipeline system grew, making gas available to many new customers, the price of gas was held down by these long-term contracts. The increased availability of natural gas combined with its low price stimulated consumption.

Finally, the shift in priorities during the 1960s, which elevated environmental quality, and especially air quality, to the level of a broadly accepted national goal, augmented the demand for natural gas relative to other fuels.

Table 2-3
Distribution of New Contract Commitments between Interstate and Intrastate Natural Gas Producers, Permian Basin Area, 1966–1970

Year	Percentage Committed Interstate	Percentage Committed Intrastate
1966	83.7	16.3
1967	78.2	21.8
1968	12.8	87.2
1969	16.7	83.3
1970 (six months)	9.1	90.9

Source: Robert B. Helms, *Natural Gas Regulation: An Evaluation of FPC Price Controls* (Washington, D.C.: American Enterprise Institute, 1974), p. 45.

Government Regulation. The chief justification for government intervention in the natural gas market is the Natural Gas Act of 1937 and the interpretation given to that act by the 1954 Supreme Court decision in the case of *Phillips Petroleum Company* v. *Wisconsin*. The Court's finding was that the Federal Power Commission had the authority to regulate the price of natural gas at the wellhead if that gas was destined for use in another state. After some indecision about how to carry out its responsibilities, the FPC began in 1960 to regulate natural gas prices, setting different prices for different producing regions. In the mid-1970s this rate system was changed, largely because of the general belief that the natural gas shortages of that time were caused by the price regulation. The new price was set at 50 cents per thousand cubic feet nationwide, from which it would increase at a regular pace in the following years.

Many observers attribute the present natural gas supply problems more to this history of federal price regulation than to inadequate resources—a view shared even by some of those authorized to enforce such regulation. Richard L. Dunham, chairman of the Federal Power Commission, assessed the problem as follows:

> There is today a shortage of natural gas in the interstate market, primarily because of the low price of interstate gas relative to the intrastate markets and to alternative fuels.
>
> The Federal Power Commission cannot eliminate these disparities through its power to set wellhead prices for interstate gas. The price established must be "just and reasonable." The courts have interpreted this standard to mean that the Commission is tied to a historical cost base plus a return on capital.
>
> We do not have authority to determine the just and reasonable price on other standards such as commodity value or market price. Such a basis provides neither the incentive for costly future drilling, nor a recognition of proper pricing in relation to alternate fuels.[32]

Why, then, should the government regulate natural gas prices at all? Granted that a Supreme Court decision said it is within the commission's *jurisdiction* to do so, another more recent lower court decision suggests that the commission is not *required* to regulate those prices directly.[33]

The traditional economic justification for the regulation of an industry begins with the premise that the industry is dominated by a small number of firms (oligopoly) or composed of a single firm (monopoly). Oligopolistic or monopolistic industries attempting to maximize their profits will set a higher price for their products and allow fewer of them onto the market than they would if they were competitive. Clearly this type of industry structure works to the disadvantage of the consumer. It also leads to a misallocation of resources throughout the economy and thus is not in the best interests of society. For these reasons, industries that are oligopolistic or monopolistic are frequently regulated by the government, the idea being to force them to produce and sell at the levels that would prevail if they had competition. Whether the natural gas market is monopolistic is subject to dispute however.

Natural Gas Policy Options. Government has a number of policy options in the case of natural gas. Three of the most often suggested are deregulation, importing liquefied gas, and leasing the outer continental shelf.

Deregulate the gas industry. One long-term policy for solving the gas shortage might be to deregulate producers. An important question to consider in analyzing this option is whether the higher prices that would result from deregulation would lead to greater supplies of gas. This question is difficult to answer because of the problem of how the market would respond to deregulated prices. To explore and develop gas deposits requires large investments from producers, investments that are deterred by uncertainty as to how well they are likely to pay off. Although one might think there would be less uncertainty under the present regulated price system than under an unregulated regime, some observers have raised arguments to the contrary. They contend that gas producers tend to discount whatever price the government approves. On the one hand, the government has the power, and has used it in the past, to reduce previously approved rates. On the other hand, producers may expect the government to approve higher prices sometime in the future—a possibility that may encourage them to slow present production. Removing these uncertainties by deregulating the wellhead price of gas would tend to increase the production of gas, though the strength of this tendency would depend on the weight producers actually attach to these factors.

An alternative to complete and abrupt deregulation would be for the regulatory commission to exempt production of new gas from price ceilings, while continuing the price controls on existing wells. Although this might lead to some waste—if gas from old wells would be profitable only under higher prices it might not be extracted—it would presumably encourage the exploration, development, and sale of new gas, which is what is needed at present. Gradually, as old wells ceased to produce, the entire industry would be decontrolled.

Import liquefied natural gas. Another long-term policy to deal with the gas shortage would be to increase imports of liquefied natural gas (LNG). The United States imports little natural gas at present; in 1974 imports accounted for less than 4 percent of domestic natural gas consumption. Most of these imports come via pipelines from Canada and Mexico, but a small portion consists of imported LNG.

To produce LNG the temperature of the gas is lowered, which converts it to liquid form and reduces its volume so that it can be economically transported by ship. Liquefied gas, however, is much more expensive than domestic natural gas. In some instances the price delivered to utilities is likely to be two to four times as high as for domestic gas. This would undoubtedly exceed any price increases that might result from deregulating the wellhead price of natural gas. Certain eastern cities have already had to resort to it, however, during gas shortages.

Leasing the outer continental shelf (OCS). Relying on offshore production of natural gas is a further option for meeting the gas shortage (although since gas from the outer continental shelf is subject to federal regulation, this option might have to be used in conjunction with one or more of those discussed above). In 1973 less than 3 percent of the OCS had been adequately mapped for purposes of determining its resource potential, and government actually had leased less than 1.5 percent to producers for oil and gas production.

The lead time is such that it will take eight years before the East coast benefits from any Atlantic gas production that is initiated, so that the earliest the East coast could receive gas from this source, if current policy continues, is 1986.

Debating the options. Clearly the liveliest political issue has been the first option, deregulation. Among those who oppose deregulation are Congressman Donald M. Fraser, who proposes instead "a firm and uniform pricing policy for *all* domestic natural gas supplies." Fraser contends that higher prices would not bring forth greater supplies of natural gas, citing an FPC report which concluded that "conventional U.S. gas production has reached its peak and will be declining for the indefinite future."[34] He also sees a lack of "workable competition" in the natural gas industry, resulting from a combination of factors including the allegedly noncompetitive nature of the major gas producers and the fact that much gas must be transported in pipelines. All of this, Fraser avers, means that deregu-

lation would not result in more gas, only gas at a higher price.

Leonard Woodcock, president of the United Automobile Workers, favors a similar approach. He stresses two key points:

It must be emphasized that there will be a continuing need for regulation of natural gas prices. Such regulation is needed for two purposes: to prevent monopolistic profiteering and to prevent windfall profits.

The monopolistic structure of the industry concerns us greatly. In many cases only one or two long-distance pipelines are available to distribute gas from a particular production area. In the major gas-producing regions of the country, the eight largest producers control between 62 percent and 100 percent of the gas reserves not yet committed to sale. Rather than actively compete with one another, these companies often collaborate together on joint economic ventures . . .

The current artificial distinction between interstate and intrastate marketing should be ended. *Federal regulation should apply to all natural gas, whether or not it is transported across state lines.*

Serious economic distortions are occurring as a result of the present segmentation of the market for natural gas. Producers have great incentive to divert supplies to the intrastate market. The FPC helped aggravate the shortage on the interstate market by making it easier to do just this. Most potential users within the producing states can obtain new supplies at a high price, while potential new users in other states cannot obtain supplies at any price.[35]

Disagreeing with this assessment are a number of economists and other observers of the natural gas industry. Patricia Starratt, in a Senate staff analysis, has reviewed the pertinent studies on the subject and finds:

The field market for natural gas is described as workably (effectively) competitive. Support for this view is drawn from analyses of field market behavior before regulation; bidding relationships in OCS lease sales; the widely divergent bids on acreage which depend on individual company evaluations; the pricing patterns in the intrastate market (which is unregulated by the FPC), and from the fact that prices in the intrastate market were relatively stable (though higher than in the interstate market) until the lack of available supply began to affect the intrastate market as well as the interstate market.

Data on the market structure also is utilized to support the view that producers are competitive. The possibility of joint bidding and joint ventures facilitates ease of entry, and because new companies can with ease enter the supply market, prices cannot be set at "monopoly levels." . . . In terms of concentration ratios . . . half of the industries in the United States are less competitive than the natural gas production industry.[36]

Coal

How extensively coal will be used in the future depends almost entirely on how successfully and how soon increasing supplies of other energy resources can be developed. The United States has sufficient coal reserves, it is agreed, to last several hundred years at present consumption rates. Yet until the future availability of oil and gas and the status of alternative sources of energy become more certain, it will not be clear how important a part coal will play in meeting our future energy demands. Using coal has certain disadvantages, none insurmountable, but all costly to overcome. Thus, if sufficient supplies of oil and gas are available, coal very likely will not take on a larger role in supplying energy over the next ten to fifteen years.

Coal Supplies. Of the major energy sources, coal is the only one in which the United States is at present fully self-sufficient. In 1974 annual production of coal was 596.0 million tons, 10 percent of which was exported.[37] The country's demonstrated coal reserve base was 434 billion tons, with eastern underground coal accounting for 38 percent, western underground 30 percent, eastern surface 8 percent, and western surface 24 percent. Forty percent of this total reserve base is on federal government land.[38]

The prospect of obtaining large amounts of future energy from the abundant supplies of western coal has attracted considerable attention. A greater portion of western than of eastern coal lies near the surface, and it has the additional advantage of having a low sulphur content. It also has a low heat yield per ton, however, which makes transportation costs per Btu relatively high. The economic pros and cons of supplying a large part of the energy demands of distant industrial centers with such coal have not yet been settled.

A second factor that dampens some of the enthusiasm about coal is the ambiguity of coal reserve figures. When coal reserves are compared with oil and natural gas reserves, it appears that coal is abundant. In large part, however, this reflects the different ways the two types of fossil fuels are measured.

Typical proved reserve figures [for oil] have been well characterized . . . as working inventories. They include only the amount of minerals that have been discovered and made ready for exploitation in quantities sufficient to support current production . . . In contrast, coal reserves are estimated on the basis of inferences from surface geological exploration . . . These figures do not represent only developed coal resources but also represent an effort to estimate those that might be developed in the future.[39]

It is probably fair to say that at least some of the endorsement often given to coal stems from an uncritical evaluation of the reserve figures.

Coal Use. At present, coal has two major uses: electricity generation and iron production, sometimes called "coking." In 1974 electricity generation accounted for 71 percent of total coal consumption in the United States. By that year, the amount of coal used for most other purposes had either declined from earlier levels or remained the same (see table 2-4). The decrease in these other uses resulted mostly from the decline in price of coal's major competitors, oil and gas. Another factor has been the increased concern about air pollution, which has resulted in the outright prohibition of coal for certain uses, such as home heating.

As a source of electric power, coal competes with natural gas, nuclear energy, and petroleum. Electric utilities have demonstrated an ability in the past to switch from one to another of these fuels in response to changes in price and availability. For example, following the federal government's decision in the early 1970s to ease the restrictions on importing residual fuel oil, electricity generation plants in New England switched from coal to oil. Similarly, some electric utility companies located in the western states turned to coal-fired plants when they were denied permission to build more hydroelectric projects. The factors that restrict the use of coal are price, environmental regulations, and the degree to which electricity can be substituted for other energy sources.

Policy Issues. "When compared to oil and gas, relative abundance of domestic supplies is the *only* virtue that can be claimed for coal," writes Richard Mancke.[40] Among the problems of coal use are its dangers to the health and safety of miners, environmental abuse from strip mining, transportation problems, its unsuitability for most purposes other than electricity generation and coking, and sulphur dioxide emissions. Most of these issues are related: if ways could be found

Table 2-4
U.S. Consumption and Exports of Bituminous Coal
(thousands of tons)

Year	Electric Power Utilities	Railroads	Coking	Other Domestic Uses	Total U.S. Consumption	Exports
1946	68,743	110,166	83,288	238,189	500,386	41,197
1950	88,262	60,969	103,845	201,126	454,202	25,468
1955	140,550	15,473	107,377	160,012	423,412	51,277
1960	173,982	2,102	81,015	123,431	380,429	36,541
1965	242,729	—[a]	94,779	121,656	459,164	50,181
1970	318,921	—[a]	96,009	100,689	515,619	70,994
1972	348,612	—[a]	87,272	83,892	519,776	55,960
1974	390,068	—[a]	89,747	72,894	552,709	59,926

[a]No longer reported separately.

Source: Richard L. Gordon, "Coal—The Swing Fuel," in *Energy Supply and Government Policy,* ed. Robert J. Ralter and William Vogely (Ithaca, N.Y.: Cornell University Press, 1976), p. 199.

to convert coal cheaply and cleanly to gas or liquid form, for example, then transportation difficulties, pollution hazards, and the problems in using coal for internal combustion engines would all be reduced or effectively eliminated.

Strip mining. From 1965 to 1973 the amount of coal produced by surface mining increased from less than 200 million to nearly 300 million tons. Underground mining over that same period accounted for nearly a constant amount of total production, roughly 300 million tons each year.[41]

Surface or strip mining is so called because it involves stripping away the earth covering a vein of coal, as opposed to digging a mine below the surface into the vein. Strip mining is the cheapest way to mine layers near the earth's surface, partly because it allows a greater percentage of the coal to be recovered. It is also safer than underground mining, and, as already mentioned, it extracts low-sulphur coal.

Strip mining does, however, have serious drawbacks. The main one is the damage it causes to the earth's surface: it destroys vegetation, thereby increasing the danger of erosion as well as eliminating refuge for birds and animals, and leaves a huge scar. The damage can be rectified in most cases, but only over time and at considerable expense. This extra cost may or may not be reflected in the price of coal. Other problems, especially in the western states, include the pollution by strip mining of valuable ground water, and the difficulty of growing new vegetation to replace what the mines have destroyed when water is as scarce as it is in the western coal regions (states such as Montana, North Dakota, Wyoming, and Colorado). At present, most major coal-mining states have laws re-

quiring reclamation of strip-mined land. There is some controversy, however, about how well these laws are observed and enforced.

Transportation. There are several ways of transporting coal from the western coal fields where much of the United States' unexploited reserves lie. Moving the coal to electricity generating plants in other areas of the country can be done by railroad. In 1973, 372 million tons of coal, or 63 percent of total domestic production, were moved by rail for at least part of the distance between the mine and their ultimate destination. A number of alternatives have been proposed, however, which are claimed either to cost less or to solve both transportation and pollution problems.

One scheme would generate electricity right at the mine mouth, although this has the disadvantage that electricity cannot be efficiently transmitted over long distances. Another proposal, one that has been widely suggested, is that the coal be converted to either a combustible gas or liquid, either of which could be moved through pipelines the same way crude oil and natural gas are. Economical processes for converting coal into such synthetic fuels are still in the developmental stage, however.

A more immediate practical variation on this proposal is that the coal be pulverized, mixed with water, and moved through pipelines. In fact, such "slurry" pipelines already exist at a number of locations in the United States and elsewhere, transporting coal as well as various minerals, such as limestone. One argument in favor of this plan is that it requires fewer tons of water per ton of coal than either gasification of coal or on-site electricity generation.[42] At present, the two coal slurry pipelines in the United States—the Black Mesa pipeline in Arizona and the Ohio pipeline which runs from southeast Ohio to Lake Erie—are declared successful by their advocates.[43]

Estimates of the costs of slurry pipelines vary. The Association of American Railroads, the chief competitor of pipelines, cites Department of Interior estimates that place pipeline costs per ton at $3.06, whereas rail costs are said to fall between $1.06 and $3.50. "There is a very narrow spread between various methods of moving coal and coal energy," according to Harry J. Breithaupt of the Association of American Railroads.[44] Defenders of the pipeline idea, on the other hand, claim that both cost and environmental advantages favor slurry pipelines. The Federal Energy Office concluded in 1974 that "slurry pipelines are economical to operate and have significant environmental advantages over more traditional modes of transport. They are safe, silent, and run underground."[45]

Air pollution. One of the major disadvantages to coal use is the damage it inflicts on air quality. Several methods of combating this problem have been proposed or tried, none so far with satisfactory results. Scrubber systems have deen developed which attempt to trap sulphur, the key pollutant from coal, but they are still too costly and prone to malfunction to be used on a wide scale. It is also possible to clean coal before burning it, but the techniques so far developed for doing so are too expensive to be practical.

One suggestion, already mentioned as a solution to the problem of transporting coal, is that coal be transformed into a liquid or gas. If this were possible at a reasonable cost, coal could be used to heat homes and power vehicles. Richard Gordon points out that "the rise of coal synthesis in any case is possible only so long as the cartel of oil producing countries remains effective. A collapse of the cartel would make imported oil the cheapest energy source."[46]

A similar argument is advanced by Edward Mitchell, who contends that gasification of coal is looked to as a solution only because natural gas is unavailable, and unavailable only because of federal government price controls. Mitchell believes that instead of spending money to convert coal to gas, we should work to bring about more rational gas pricing policies.[47] Coal conversion is only a second-best alternative to other remedies of the oil and gas supply problems.

Coal's Future. Despite the difficulties increased use of coal will very likely present, such a course is advocated by both the Carter administration and a number of

independent organizations. The president's National Energy Plan contends:

Coal will meet the greatest portion of increased U.S. energy needs. A comprehensive coal research and development program is a high priority . . . In the short term, most coal will continue to be burned directly. Hence, the highest immediate priority is the development of more effective, economical pollution controls standards.[48]

However, as the plan notes, none of the various possible solutions to the problems involved with burning coal is yet fully developed, nor is there any certainty that a major breakthrough is imminent.

The Committee for Economic Development also favors increased coal development. It advocates "use of incentives as well as disincentives, including permitting the immediate depreciation for tax purposes of new investment in equipment needed to facilitate the burning of coal."[49]

Increased use of coal, whether in solid form or converted, is not universally supported, however. Richard Mancke contends that it would be an inefficient use of resources:

In view of these costs and the availability of other secure and cheaper sources of lower-polluting energy, the recent emphasis on developing our coal supplies seems unwise. Over at least the next fifteen years it would be much wiser to take steps encouraging greater oil and gas flows from Alaska, Canada, and the offshore areas.[50]

Nuclear and Other Sources of Energy

Turning to sources of energy not now in widespread use, one quickly finds what is imaginable outpacing what is possible. There is, as the saying goes, many a slip 'twixt the cup and the lip. One can see this even in the case of nuclear energy. While nuclear power has proven to be one source of electricity, it is clear after nearly twenty years of use that the original hopes for nuclear power as a solution to the energy problem were wildly optimistic. Now, as we consider other proposed sources of energy, we should take care to assess their technological and economic viability. Some research and development effort is probably justified to develop alternatives to oil and natural gas; yet experience in energy research in the past does not give ground for more than guarded optimism.

Nuclear Energy. Only 4 percent of the United States' electricity at present comes from nuclear power plants.

Since it takes at least five to seven years to build a plant, and several years to obtain permission to undertake construction, nuclear energy is certainly not a source of energy that can be counted on to meet new demands in the short term. Under the most optimistic forecasts, nuclear energy would not supply more than 20 percent of the electricity consumed in the United States by the year 1990.[51]

Nuclear plants now in commercial operation are of the type called "light water reactors." These reactors use uranium fuel, and energy stored in atomic bonds is freed as a result of neutron bombardment. The energy released this way is used to heat water; the water in turn is used either directly to drive a steam turbine or indirectly to heat yet another water system by means of a shared heat exchanger.

Two problems arise in the use of light water reactors. First, the nuclear reaction itself throws off harmful radiation, and it is possible that through a reactor "meltdown" (a malfunction of the reactor's cooling system), a nonatomic explosion could throw radioactive material across the surrounding countryside to be carried off by the winds. Second, there is great question as to what should be done with the spent fuel. Some of it may remain radioactive for a thousand years, and a small portion (plutonium) for 24 thousand years.

Aside from these problems, there is the danger that a terrorist group, for example, could find a way to intercept enriched nuclear fuel and use it to make an atomic bomb. It is widely believed that aside from getting the fuel, building a nuclear bomb would not be extremely difficult.

The light water reactor is not the only possible type of nuclear reactor. The liquid metal fast breeder reactor, about which much dispute has arisen, would use liquid sodium instead of water as a coolant and would operate at much higher temperatures. It has the advantage of using a much greater percentage of the energy potential in its fuel than does the light water reactor, because it runs at higher temperatures and thus can be made more efficient. The fast breeder reactor uses fusion power, a rather different type of nuclear energy, which entails bringing together two hydrogen atoms to form a helium atom. This is, in its basics, the same type of reaction as that from which the sun's energy derives. By all accounts, this nuclear reactor is still very much in the early stage of development.

Although the fast breeder reactor is technologically somewhat easier to develop than is the fusion reactor, it is nevertheless not generally regarded as adaptable to commercial use. A number of studies have concluded that the costs of the research and development program and of the operation of the plants would be too great to justify an intensive effort to develop this source. The Atomic Energy Commission, on the other hand, concludes on the basis of its own cost-benefit analyses that the fast breeder would be an economically worthwhile undertaking.[52]

Although the record of existing light water reactors has been good, there is still an understandable concern about their safety. According to a study conducted by Norman Rasmussen at the request of the Atomic Energy Commission, a meltdown in most cases would cause only minor property damage and pose only a small threat to health, although the unlikely possibility does exist of much greater damage.[53]

Besides working to increase nuclear plant safety, another nuclear policy option is locating reactors only at remote sites. The electricity generated by these plants, in addition to being transmitted to populated areas, could be used to split water molecules; the resulting hydrogen and oxygen then could be shipped via pipelines to places where energy is needed. Hydrogen is an exceptionally clean fuel—the only byproduct when it is burned is water.

Nuclear fuel—uranium—is relatively abundant. In 1974 uranium reserves in the United States amounted to the equivalent of 1,920 trillion Btu, compared with between 400 and 500 trillion for natural gas and petroleum. (Total undiscovered recoverable resources of *each* of these three energy sources—oil, gas, and uranium—were estimated to be between 1,000 and 2,000 trillion Btu.) Keeping in mind the much lower fraction of total energy uranium is expected to provide in the next twenty years than oil and gas, it appears we can be less concerned about reserves of nuclear fuel than other sources of energy.

Hydroelectric Power. About 14 percent of the electricity used in the United States at present comes from hydroelectric projects, such as dams which harness the water power of rivers to generate electricity. The basic constraint on further expansion of this source is that not a great deal of unexploited capacity exists. It has been estimated that about 10 quadrillion Btu more per year could be generated by hydro power; present output is roughly 3 quadrillion Btu per year, and it comes from the most favorable sites. If prices for coal and oil continue to rise, it may become remunerative to build hydroelectric projects at locations previously passed over. Present federal policy calls for the Army Corps of Engineers and other agencies with responsibility in this area to look for additional dam sites.

Geothermal Energy. Geothermal energy is the natural heat of the earth transferred to the surface in water or steam. Extracting geothermal power is now practical only in areas with natural high-pressure steam reserves, which are mostly in the far western United States. At present, geothermal energy is used for electric power generation, space heating, and industrial processing. Geothermal power is estimated to be less costly than fossil fuels and nuclear power, and slightly more expensive than hydropower. Because of the concentration of resources in the western states, geothermal energy could only contribute significantly to power needs within that region.

The major geothermal field in the United States is Geysers Field in California, which provides about one-third of the electric power used in San Francisco. The nation's existing geothermal capacity is less than 1 percent of our total generating capacity from all sources.[54]

In 1970 Congress passed the Geothermal Steam Act, which authorizes leasing of public lands to producers interested in developing geothermal resources. President Carter also has encouraged the development of geothermal energy in his Energy Plan, which proposes legislation that would extend the same special tax treatment to geothermal drilling as now applies to oil and gas, and also proposes making more research and development funds available.[55] There are, however, technological problems that must be solved before geothermal power can be used on a wide scale. In addition, potential environmental problems range from air and water pollution to subsidence of land or seismic disturbance caused by pumping.

Shale Oil. Within the United States are eleven million acres of land—almost three-fourths of it federally owned—containing oil shale deposits with a potential for commercial use. Possibly two trillion barrels of oil are embedded in the bituminous shale or brown coal on this land. Although it is sometimes asserted that present world prices make shale oil development a worthwhile undertaking, this has yet to be demonstrated. Uncertainty over energy policy and future prices is felt to have deterred progress in this area.

Burning fuels refined from shale oil would, it has been suggested, have little ill effect on the environment, for such fuels contain almost no sulfur or ash. The production of shale oil could have an undesirable impact on the environment, however.

Solar Energy. Solar energy is derived directly from the sun, and most experts say it would be the least damaging to the environment of all fuels. It has been estimated that if 2 percent of the land area of the United States were used to collect solar energy and "if the conversion efficiency to useful energy were to be 10 percent, solar energy alone would allow a five-fold expansion in America's use of energy."[56] Present methods of utilizing solar energy are satisfactory for space and water heating, although for most conventionally constructed homes, adapting to solar energy would cost more than installing conventional systems. Current federal policy proposals call for tax credits to both homeowners and businesses based on how much solar heating equipment they install. Other solar technologies, specifically the ones aimed at generating electricity directly from solar radiation, are in preliminary phases of development and have found application only in specialized uses accounting for a tiny fraction of total energy consumption.

President Carter's National Energy Plan urges that the use of sources such as those mentioned in this section be increased. "The use of nonconventional sources of energy must be vigorously expanded. Relatively clean or inexhaustible sources of energy offer a hopeful prospect of supplementing conventional energy sources in this country."[57]

John C. DeHaven, an engineer-chemist at the Rand Corporation, makes a point concerning solar energy that can be applied to a number of unconventional energy sources: "One suspects that most solar energy applications are neither financially nor economically attractive in view of anticipated costs for other energy resources. Previous experience has shown that where conventional fuels are expensive, commercial sources of solar energy devices become available."[58]

Good policy in the area of unconventional resources depends on two things: the ability of businesses (some of them engaged solely or primarily in energy research) to be innovative in energy use, and the degree to which government can provide efficient research and development efforts when businesses cannot.

NOTES

[1] U.S., Congress, House, Committee on Interstate and Foreign Commerce, *Basic Energy Data,* 94th Cong., 1st sess., 1975, p. 135.

[2] Ibid.

[3] U.S., Department of Commerce and U.S., Bureau of the Census, *Statistical Abstract of the United States, 1977* (Washington, D.C., 1977), p. 753.

[4] Ibid., p. 752.

[5] Motor Vehicle Manufacturers Association, *Motor Vehicle Facts and Figures '76,* Detroit, Mich., p. 29.

[6] Milton Russell, "Energy," in *Setting National Priorities: The 1978 Budget,* ed. Joseph A. Pechman (Washington, D.C.: Brookings Institution, 1977), table 10-3, p. 331.

[7] Dennis Epple, *Petroleum Discoveries and Government Policy* (Cambridge, Mass.: Ballinger Publishing Co., 1975), p. 11. The preceding discussion on oil exploration draws heavily on this book; see pp. 5–11.

[8] In Edward J. Mitchell, *U.S. Energy Policy: A Primer* (Washington, D.C.: American Enterprise Institute, 1976), pp. 31–32.

[9] Ibid., p. 32.

[10] Ibid., p. 35.

[11] John C. Fisher, *Energy Crises in Perspective* (New York: John Wiley & Sons, 1974), pp. 28–29.

[12] For an extended discussion of these points see ibid., chapter 4.

[13] House, Committee on Interstate and Foreign Commerce, *Basic Energy Data,* p. 126. The figures in the text come from a different source than those in figure 2-1 and also are classified somewhat differently.

[14] Ibid., p. 67.

[15] Russell, "Energy," tables 10-1 and 10-3, pp. 319 and 331.

[16] Hendrik Houthakker, *The World Price of Oil* (Washington, D.C.: American Enterprise Institute, 1976), p. 1.

[17] Mitchell, *U.S. Energy Policy,* p. 49.

[18] U.S., Executive Office of the President, *The National Energy Plan* (Washington, D.C., 1977), p. xi.

[19] Melvin R. Laird, *Energy—A Crisis in Public Policy* (Washington, D.C.: American Enterprise Institute, 1977), p. 6.

[20] Ibid., p. 7.

[21] Walter J. Mead, *An Economic Appraisal of President Carter's Energy Program* (Los Angeles: International Institute for Economic Research, 1977), pp. 18–19.

[22] *New York Times,* April 13, 1978, "Letters to the Editor."

[23] Organization of the Petroleum Exporting Countries, *Annual Statistical Bulletin,* 1976, p. iii.

[24] U.S., Congress, Senate, Committee on the Judiciary, *The Petroleum Industry,* Part I, 94th Cong., 1st sess., September 23, 1976, p. 3.

[25] Ibid., Part II, pp. 21–22.

[26] Ibid.

[27] Morris A. Adelman, "The Changing Structure of Big International Oil," in *Oil, Divestiture, and National Security,* ed. Frank N. Trager (New York: Crane, Russak & Co., 1977), p. 10.

[28] David J. Teece, "Vertical Integration in the U.S. Oil Industry," in *Vertical Integration in the Oil Industry,* ed. Edward J. Mitchell (Washington, D.C.: American Enterprise Institute, 1976), pp. 181–182.

[29] House, Committee on Interstate and Foreign Commerce, *Basic Energy Data,* p. 154.

[30] Ibid., p. 157.

[31] Stephen Breyer and Paul M. MacAvoy, "The Natural Gas Shortage and the Regulation of Natural Gas Producers," *Harvard Law Review,* vol. 86, April 1973, p. 975.

[32] U.S., Congress, House, Committee on Interstate and Foreign Commerce, Subcommittee on Energy and Power, *Long-Term Natural Gas Legislation,* 94th Cong., 2nd sess., January 1976, p. 821.

[33] Southern Louisiana Area Rate Cases, 428 F. 2d 407, 416 n. 9 (5th Cir.), cert. denied, 400 U.S. 950 (1970).

[34] House, Committee on Interstate and Foreign Commerce, *Long-Term Natural Gas Legislation,* pp. 8 and 10.

[35] Ibid., pp. 673–674. Emphasis in original.

[36] Patricia Starratt, *Natural Gas Policy Issues and Options,* U.S. Senate staff analysis (Washington, D.C., 1973), p. 10.

[37] House, Committee on Interstate and Foreign Commerce, *Basic Energy Data,* p. 118.

[38] Ibid., pp. 164–165.

[39] Richard L. Gordon, "Coal—The Swing Fuel," in *Energy Supply and Government Policy,* ed. Robert J. Kalter and William A. Vogely (Ithaca, N.Y.: Cornell University Press, 1976), p. 194.

[40] Richard Mancke, *The Failure of U.S. Energy Policy* (New York: Columbia University Press, 1974), p. 131.

[41] House, Committee on Interstate and Foreign Com-

merce, *Basic Energy Data,* p. 173.

[42] U.S., Congress, Senate, Committee on Interior and Insular Affairs, Subcommittee on Minerals, Materials and Fuels, *Hearings on Coal Slurry Pipelines,* 93rd Cong., 2nd sess., June 11, 1974, pp. 62, 64.

[43] Ibid., p. 56.

[44] Ibid., p. 103.

[45] Ibid., p. 159.

[46] Gordon, "Coal—The Swing Fuel," p. 211.

[47] Mitchell, *U.S. Energy Policy,* p. 25.

[48] Executive Office, *National Energy Plan,* p. 68.

[49] Committee for Economic Development, Research and Policy Committee, *Key Elements of a National Energy Strategy* (New York, 1977), p. 12.

[50] Mancke, *Failure of Energy Policy,* pp. 133–134.

[51] House, Committee on Interstate and Foreign Commerce, *Basic Energy Data,* p. 106.

[52] U.S. Atomic Energy Commission, Division of Reactor Development and Technology, *Proposed Final Environmental Statement,* LMFBR, WASH-1535. For the results of a cost-benefit analysis with unfavorable results, see Brian G. Chow, *The Liquid Metal Fast Breeder Reactor: An Economic Analysis* (Washington, D.C.: American Enterprise Institute, 1975).

[53] Summarized in John F. O'Leary, "Nuclear Energy and Public Policy Issues," in *Energy Supply and Government Policy,* ed. Kalter and Vogely, p. 244.

[54] House, Committee on Interstate and Foreign Commerce, *Basic Energy Data,* p. 188.

[55] Executive Office, *National Energy Plan,* p. 78.

[56] U.S., Congress, Senate, Committee on Interior and Insular Affairs, *National Goals Symposium: Hearings on Energy and National Goals,* Part I, 92nd Cong., 2nd sess., 1971, p. 23.

[57] Executive Office, *National Energy Plan,* p. xiii.

[58] John C. DeHaven, "Energy Research and Development," in M. A. Adelman and others, *No Time to Confuse* (San Francisco: Institute for Contemporary Studies, 1975), pp. 125–126.

Chapter 3

THE CONTROL OF ENERGY DEVELOPMENT AND DISTRIBUTION

*Resolved: That the federal government should exclusively
control the development and distribution
of energy resources in the United States.*

Especially since the early 1970s, the extent to which the federal government should make decisions directly concerning the development and distribution of energy resources has been a topic of much discussion and debate. Presidents, Congress, private foundations, magazines, newspapers, and television networks have commissioned numerous investigations of matters related to this issue. Among the topics they have considered are consumption patterns and trends, energy pricing and shortages, industry competitiveness, the distributional effect of high energy prices on various income groups, environmental and safety factors, and alternative sources of energy for the future.

In 1973 the nation was abruptly made aware of its dependence upon energy when OPEC raised oil prices and the Arab nations placed a partial embargo on their oil exports. The shortages of gasoline that accompanied government price controls lasted only a few months (although the memories of waiting in line for hours for a few gallons of gasoline may last much longer); yet the nation still was faced with adjusting to the fourfold increase in the price of imported oil. Prices of alternative forms of energy also rose as people demanded more oil substitutes.

Since 1973, when the so-called energy crisis first became a major focus of public discussion, Americans have assumed that the federal government and the private sector would work to arrive at a new policy governing the development and distribution of energy resources in the United States. A new policy has not, however, been implemented. In 1977 President Carter's National Energy Plan proposed that the federal government should assume a more prominent and permanent role in the development and distribution of energy resources. Others feel that the time has come for the federal government to get out of the energy business and return control to private enterprise and consumers. The first debate proposition—that the federal government should exclusively control the development and distribution of energy resources in the United States—

suggests yet a third position, one that implies a greater role for government than even the National Energy Plan envisages.

The terms and overall specification of the debate proposition should be carefully considered. It specifies that it is the *federal government* that should be given the authority and responsibility to control the development and distribution of energy resources. The federal government consists of the Congress, the federal courts, the executive branch (including the President and the Department of Energy), and various independent agencies such as the Tennessee Valley Authority, which is a government-owned producer of electricity. Giving these bodies greater control is to be contrasted with leaving decisions about the development and distribution of energy to individuals, private firms, or state and local governmental authorities.

The term *exclusively* indicates that the authority and responsibility for *all* decisions concerning the development and distribution of energy resources are to belong to the federal government. Any developmental or distributional activities undertaken by individuals, firms, or nonfederal governmental agencies would be at the behest of, or only by the permission of, the federal government.

Control means "to exercise restraining or directing influence over,"[1] and might range from comprehensive regulation of existing producers and distributors in the various energy industries to nationalization of the energy industries and prohibition of private initiative in these areas.

Development of energy resources includes basic research to discover and develop new technologies, such as coal gasification, the liquid metal fast breeder reactor, and solar space heating; demonstrating the feasibility of new technologies by building prototype plants or demonstration models; drilling oil and natural gas wells; and building nuclear power plants.

Distribution of energy resources involves transporting oil, natural gas, coal, electricity, and other energy forms to industrial, commercial, and household users of energy, and also setting the prices at which various types of energy may be sold and the rationing mechanism, if any, by which energy resources are allocated to various users. Under the resolution, the federal government would decide who gets how much energy, how, at what prices, for what purposes, and at what time. For example, the government might simply set a price at which electricity could be sold nationally, regardless of variations in production costs, and allow anyone to purchase as much as they wanted (if available). Or the federal government might set different prices in different regions and at different times of the day. The federal government could limit quantities purchased at specified prices, or restrict the uses for which energy may be purchased. The number of ways the federal government could control the distribution of energy resources is limitless, and the methods chosen would depend upon the goals, interests, and abilities of the people running the government.

Energy resources include fossil fuels such as oil, natural gas, coal, and shale oil, plus nonfossil resources such as uranium, solar energy, wood, tides, the earth's molten core, and falling water.

General Arguments Regarding Federal Control

National gas shortages, pollution, despoilment of the environment, threats to national security posed by potential nuclear proliferation, vulnerability to blackmail or economic disruption, monopoly power in energy-producing firms, electrical blackouts, and effects of high energy prices on low-income groups are all potential reasons for the government to act to try to improve the development and distribution of energy resources in the United States. The government extensively regulates many aspects of the development and distribution of energy resources already. Some of the problems just listed have been ameliorated by the existing regulations, while other problems have been made worse or even caused by them. Few people believe that the current set of federal regulations in the energy sector is all it should be, and proposals for revisions to reflect the current and future energy situation in the United States have come from all directions. George Leland Bach has summarized the present state of affairs:

Just about everyone agrees that we need a unified national energy policy to replace our present hodge-podge of regulations. The problem is enormously complex, and any successful policy will surely have many facets. Two fundamental approaches dominate the discussion. One is increased government intervention and regulation—government controls over

what forms of energy to produce where; how the energy should be distributed; who should get it, at what prices, and for what purposes. Avoiding windfall profits for the big oil companies through higher prices is an important goal in this approach.

The other approach calls for increased use of built-in individual incentives—letting the price system do a big part of the job. This would involve letting energy prices rise as demand grows relative to supply—in order to stimulate production, to reduce use of increasingly expensive fuels for less essential purposes, and to encourage development of substitutes. Under our public utility regulation, Americans have long had the cheapest gas and electricity in the world, and very cheap oil. Little wonder we use lots and face dwindling supplies relative to demand. Under this approach, producer profits might rise sharply with higher prices, although defenders point to the large number of companies competing at all stages of energy production and distribution as substantial protection against improperly high prices.[2]

Successful support of the debate proposition calling for exclusive federal control of the development and distribution of energy resources depends on evidence showing that the alternative—relying on private enterprise and the free market price system (possibly in conjunction with limited federal, state, and local regulation)—is inferior to exclusive federal control.

President Carter, in the National Energy Plan he submitted to Congress for consideration in April 1977, proposed to move *toward* greater federal control of the development and distribution of energy resources:

The United States is at a turning point. It can choose, through piecemeal programs and policies, to continue the current state of drift. That course would require no hard decisions, no immediate sacrifices, and no adjustment to the new energy realities. That course may, for the moment, seem attractive. But, with each passing day, the nation falls farther behind in solving its energy problems. Consequently, its economic and foreign policy position weakens, its options dwindle, and the ultimate transition to stringency in oil supplies and higher oil prices becomes more difficult.

An alternative to continued drift is the comprehensive National Energy Plan.[3]

This plan presents ten principles intended as guidelines for U.S. energy policy, plus a series of specific legislative proposals for new regulations and taxes in the energy sector.

"The first principle is that the energy problem can be effectively addressed only by a Government that accepts responsibility for dealing with it comprehensively, and by a public that understands its seriousness and is ready to make necessary sacrifices."[4] According to President Carter, then, the federal government should assume responsibility for dealing with all aspects of the energy problem, which includes the development and distribution of energy resources. The features of the proposed National Energy Plan therefore may be examined by proponents and opponents of the debate proposition as an example of one form that federal control of the development and distribution of energy resources could take. In this analysis we will discuss parts of the Energy Plan, as well as other possible forms of federal control, comparing these with alternatives such as unregulated free enterprise and mixed private and governmental control.

There are many possible justifications for government intervention in energy markets: monopoly power of private firms or groups of firms, environmental concerns, public safety, issues of national security and foreign dependence, balance of payments problems, inflation, and the unacceptable burdens high energy prices impose on the poor. If we assume for the moment that there *is* a need for government intervention in energy markets, bearing in mind the interdependence of energy markets, we can compare the advantages, disadvantages, and feasibility of piecemeal or locally legislated regulations with those of ideal comprehensive federal controls and those controls likely in practice. In the discussion of the existing federal regulations of the energy industry that follows, not only the directly intended effects but many examples of secondary effects of regulations on production and distribution of energy resources are pointed out.

Monopoly Power in Energy Supply

If the individual firms in an industry have monopoly power, or if the firms in an industry can collude with one another to obtain monopoly power, then they may restrict their output in order to drive up prices for their products and thereby obtain higher profits. Curtailed output in the oil and natural gas industries, for example, would mean less oil or natural gas available for heating homes, schools, and offices, less gasoline and diesel fuel for cars and trucks, less fertilizer for farmers, and less of all the myriad of final products in which oil or natural gas is important. OPEC currently uses its monopoly power to keep prices higher than competitive levels, but it is outside the realm of control of the United States federal government. How much output domestic firms may curtail depends on the strength of their monopoly power, if any.

The higher prices monopolies are inclined to charge are considered an unfair burden on consumers. If oil or natural gas were priced monopolistically, a disproportionate share of the burden would fall on the poor, since money spent on energy generally is a larger share of the household budget in a poor family (see table 3-1). Although the exercise of monopoly power results in the use of less of the resource in question, in energy as in other fields, the likelihood of monopoly power is often thought to justify federal government intervention to protect the public interest. Before government adopts any policies intended to deal with monopoly power, the market structure, prices, and profit rates in the domestic energy industries should be examined for evidence that a monopoly exists. In general, monopoly power is considered to be present when a single firm or a small number of firms control enough of an industry's output to be able to influence market prices. Concentration ratios—that is, the percentage of total industry output, sales, or capacity held by a certain number (usually four), of the largest firms—are a common measure of potential monopoly power. Table 3-2 presents four- and eight-firm concentration ratios for the major primary energy-producing industries in the United States.

The final report by the Energy Policy Project of the

Table 3-1
Percentage of Family Income Spent on Energy

Average Annual Family Income (dollars)	Average Annual Btu per Household (millions)	Average Annual Cost per Household (dollars)	Percent of Total Annual Income Spent on Energy
2,500	207	379	15.2
8,000	294	572	7.2
14,000	403	832	5.9
24,500	478	994	4.1

Source: Ford Foundation Energy Policy Project, *A Time to Choose: America's Energy Future* (Cambridge, Mass.: Ballinger Publishing Co., 1974), p. 118.

Table 3-2
Concentration Ratios for Energy Industries in the United States

	Uranium Mining and Milling		Crude Oil Production		Petroleum Refining		Gasoline Sales		Natural Gas Production		Coal Production		Energy Production (Btu basis)	
	1955	1976	1955	1976	1955	1976	1954	1976	1955	1976	1955	1976	1955	1970
Four largest firms	79.9	57.7	18.1	25.5	33.1	32.7	31.2	29.3	21.7	23.5	17.8	25.1	11.0	21.2
Eight largest firms	99.1	71.3	30.3	40.5	57.7	56.9	54.0	49.9	33.1	35.6	25.5	34.3	19.7	35.0

Note: A concentration ratio measures the percentage of a given activity undertaken by the largest firms (usually the four or eight largest) engaged in that activity.

Sources: Ford Foundation Energy Policy Project, *A Time to Choose: America's Energy Future* (Cambridge, Mass.: Ballinger Publishing Co., 1974), p. 231; Edward J. Mitchell, ed., *Vertical Integration in the Oil Industry* (Washington, D.C.: American Enterprise Institute, 1976), p. 51; Pamela Murphy, *U.S. Petroleum Market Volumes and Market Shares* (Washington, D.C.: American Petroleum Institute, 1977), pp. 1, 28, 47; Pamela Murphy, *Concentration Levels in the Production and Reserve Holdings of Crude Oil, Natural Gas, Coal, and Uranium in the U.S., 1955–1976* (Washington, D.C.: American Petroleum Institute, 1977), pp. 8–11.

Ford Foundation assesses monopoly power in energy industries as follows:

> It is impossible to designate a precise point below which an industry can be decisively judged competitive, or above which it can be judged uncompetitive, but a rule of thumb has been formulated which says that monopoly power begins to be felt when the four largest firms account for more than 50 percent of the industry's output, or when the eight largest account for more than 70 percent. By these standards, only two elements in the energy business—the uranium mining and milling industry, and the electric generating equipment industry—are uncompetitive.[5]

Even for the two energy industries meeting the rule-of-thumb criteria for potential monopoly power, the high concentration ratios found do not necessarily imply a lack of competition. Firms *may* act competitively even if there are only a few of them in an industry. Even a single-firm industry may be competitive if it faces the threat of new competitors entering the industry. In both these energy industries, however, firms have in fact been charged with violating antitrust laws.

It has been argued that conventional concentration ratios are inadequate measures of the potential for monopoly in the petroleum industry because of its unique structure.

> The key structural feature of the petroleum industry is that virtually all of its corporate entities are extensively tied together through a very large number of joint venture arrangements and other types of intercorporate interlocks. Consequently, these firms cannot be viewed in parallel with independent unrelated market rivals in other industries.[6]

The large oil companies do engage in many joint ventures, making shared investments in pipelines and leasing federally owned land. The top twenty firms are active in all aspects of production, from drilling wells to selling to retail consumers, including the intermediate functions of transportation and refining. Most large oil companies also are engaged in the production of other forms of energy as well, including natural gas, oil shale, coal, and uranium.

One way of predicting the potential future monopoly power of the large oil companies is to investigate the extent of their control over domestic oil reserves. Table 3-3 shows that proven reserve holdings were even more concentrated than domestic production. The reliability of proven reserve estimates is low, however; and the fact that these estimates do not include yet-to-be-discovered reserves limits the confidence we should place in any conclusions drawn from the higher concentration ratios based on them. Additional evidence is required to determine whether these attributes of the market structure of energy industries might result in significant monopoly power.

To exercise monopoly power successfully over a long period, firms must be able to protect themselves from competition from new entrants into their industry. If new firms are able to enter the field without having to overcome substantial barriers, then it is impossible for their older competitors (even very large ones) to maintain high prices for longer than it takes the new firms to start production. In the oil industry, independents (firms not associated with the large oil companies) drilled 81 percent of new oil and natural gas wells in the United States and discovered 88 percent of new fields in 1977, suggesting that entry is relatively easy at least at the first stage of petroleum development.[7]

Pipeline transportation of crude oil, natural gas, and gasoline appears to be a sector of the energy industry in which there are substantial barriers against the entry of competing firms. Because the unit costs of pipelines

Table 3-3
Company Shares of Domestic Crude Oil Production and Proven Reserves, 1976
(percent)

Company	Domestic Production	Domestic Proven Reserves
Exxon USA	8.3	10.2
Texaco	6.3	7.2
Shell	5.5	4.8
Standard of Indiana	5.5	5.4
Gulf	4.1	3.2
Socal	3.8	3.8
ARCO	3.7	7.3
Mobil	3.3	2.5
Getty	2.9	4.5
Sun	2.6	2.3
Phillips	2.5	1.5
Union	2.4	1.5
Continental	2.0	1.3
Cities Service	2.0	1.1
Marathon	1.8	2.3
City of Long Beach	1.1	NA
Amerada Hess	1.0	0.9
Tenneco	0.9	0.6
Louisiana Land	0.8	0.4
Superior	NA	0.3
Standard of Ohio	NA	13.9
Top four	25.5	38.7
Top eight	40.5	57.3

NA: Not available.

Source: Pamela Murphy, *Concentration Levels in the Production and Reserve Holdings of Crude Oil, Natural Gas, Coal, and Uranium in the U.S., 1955–1976* (Washington, D.C.: American Petroleum Institute, 1977), pp. 20, 39.

fall as the volume of crude oil or refined products to be transported rises, what is called a "natural" monopoly results (except for potential competition from alternate modes of transport, including railroad tank cars, trucks, and barges). At present, according to Edward J. Mitchell, "The Interstate Commerce Commission (ICC) has the responsibility for ensuring that interstate pipelines do not discriminate against nonowners. It attempts to do this by regulationg rates and assuring that all shippers are granted access."[8]

The high capital investments required are thought to be an important barrier to entry in refining, but "there were forty-seven entrants into U.S. refining between 1950 and 1972 and thirteen new entrants between 1972 and 1975."[9] Entry into marketing of petroleum products such as gasoline or fuel oil generally requires relatively small investment, and that area is generally regarded as open to newcomers.

Domestic interstate prices of natural gas and domestically produced oil are currently controlled by the federal government at levels below the prices of imports. In the case of oil, at least, the import price would be the domestic price as well in the absence of controls. Therefore there is little we can ascertain from current domestic prices about the extent of monopoly power in the largest firms in the energy industry.

Monopoly power in the energy industries would be indicated if profits were sustained at above-normal rates. Table 3-4 presents average profits as a percent of invested capital for the twenty largest U.S. petroleum firms (ranked according to 1971 sales) over the period 1967 to 1972 and also for 1973. The average rate of

Table 3-4
Profits as a Percentage of Invested Capital for the Twenty Largest U.S. Petroleum Firms

Firm (ranked according to 1971 sales)	Average Profit Rate (1967–1972)	Profit Rate (1973)
Exxon	12.3	19.4
Mobil Oil	10.7	16.0
Texaco	13.8	17.6
Gulf Oil	10.4	14.8
Standard Oil of California (Chevron)	10.4	15.7
Standard Oil of Indiana (Amoco)	9.7	13.1
Shell Oil	10.6	11.1
Atlantic Richfield	8.4	7.8
Continental Oil	10.1	14.5
Tenneco[a]	11.2	NA
Occidental Petroleum	14.2	7.2
Phillips Petroleum	8.4	12.4
Union Oil of California	9.2	10.1
Sun Oil	9.5	10.8
Ashland Oil	11.6	18.2
Standard Oil of Ohio (Sohio)	8.2	6.8
Getty Oil	8.5	9.1
Marathon Oil	11.4	15.9
Clark Oil	15.2	33.4
Commonwealth Oil Refining	11.5	20.5
Oil industry composite	10.8	15.1
Average for all manufacturing (1967–1971)	10.8	

NA: Not available.

[a]Tenneco is a conglomerate with only about 15 percent of revenues derived from oil operations (*Economic Report of the President*, January 1973, p. 280).

Source: Ford Foundation Energy Policy Project, *A Time to Choose: America's Energy Future* (Cambridge, Mass.: Ballinger Publishing Co., 1974), p. 237.

return on capital for these twenty largest firms in the oil industry was the same as the average rate of return for all manufacturing industries during the same period. The evidence from rates of return, then, indicates that there is no more monopoly power in the petroleum industry than in manufacturing as a whole.

Profits of petroleum companies increased in 1973 and would have increased by a larger amount if prices of domestic output had not been controlled. The increase in profits was largely a result of the OPEC supply restraints and resulting higher prices. *Business Week* notes, ''Recently, thanks to the quadrupling of world oil prices since 1973, the industry's return on invested capital has jumped 30%. Last year [1977] the fifteen largest oil companies earned $10.7 billion after taxes, for a 14% average return on invested capital.''[10] This return, however, was lower than the 15 percent average return earned by the 1,745 leading manufacturing corporations.[11] Still, whether the oil industry's higher profits since 1973 are exorbitant or not, and whether the government should take any action about ''windfall'' profits, were the subject of considerable public debate.

One result of the higher profits was an increase in investments by the energy industry. According to the National Energy Plan, ''From 1973 through 1975, the United States invested $112 billion in plant and equipment to produce energy, about 35 percent of all such expenditures throughout the economy. Previously, the share of investment going to energy production had ranged between 25 and 30 percent.''[12] Most economists would regard that increased investment as evidence of the private enterprise systems responding well and in a socially beneficial manner to changes in economic conditions. The view expressed in the National Energy Plan, on the other hand, was that the increased investment in energy production drew off a disportionate share of capital from other sectors.

Stimulating Private Research and Development

Research and development aimed at discovering new ways to produce energy are necessary to assure the United States of future long-term supplies. The *Wall Street Journal* notes that the Carter administration is drawing up preliminary plans for ''the investment of hundreds of millions of dollars in Energy Department funds, loan guarantees and possibly small tax incentives to develop substitutes for oil and natural gas that can be used in the years between 1985 and the end of the century.''[13] But how deeply and how broadly the federal government should become involved in energy research and development remains an important policy issue to be decided by the Congress and the people as well as the executive branch.

If the production and distribution of energy resources are left to the private sector, then we will have to rely on market incentives to induce private enterprise to conduct research to develop alternative energy sources. Among these incentives could be profits at the uncontrolled price, additional price rises, or perhaps the likelihood that prices will rise if no research is undertaken. If the federal government chooses to continue to control domestic prices at current levels, this removes much of the incentive for the private sector to undertake research to develop new techniques for extracting oil and natural gas from hard-to-recover deposits or from coal. Even if energy prices are decontrolled, however, there are several reasons why the private sector might still make inadequate investments in energy research and development. As John E. Tilton has noted:

The output of R&D is new knowledge and technology. Unlike the output of a steel furnace, an automobile assembly line, or most other production processes, new knowledge and technology possess the unusual quality that they can be sold or given away and still used by the transmitting organization. Indeed, because of imperfections in the market for new knowledge and technology due in large part to their nature, firms can rarely prevent some dissemination of their R&D results, even if they try to do so through secrecy or patents. As a result, the social benefits from R&D often appreciably exceed the private benefits.[14]

Firms will engage in research and development when they expect to earn a profit by doing so. For some projects, however, many of the advances in new technology or production techniques are easily copied by other firms. Since the benefits of a successful research and development program may go to many firms, an individual firm has little incentive to bear the entire cost of such a program itself. The result may be that private companies are not willing to make sufficient investments in energy research and development to guarantee that our future national energy needs will be met in the most efficient manner.

One way the government could address this problem would be by strengthening the private sector's incentives to do research and development. It could accomplish this by broadening existing patent laws, granting firms the right to benefit exclusively from their discoveries, lengthening the life of patents beyond the current seventeen years, and having the courts at all levels of government enforce the rights of firms to charge royalties to anyone using the new technology they develop. Another possibility is for government to encourage greater cooperation among firms and industrywide trade associations to conduct research and development. This would give greater incentives to the private sector to make R&D expenditures, since a greater proportion of the returns to research and development investments could be appropriated by industry. Present federal antitrust policies regulating mergers or cooperation among firms would have to be revised. A potential drawback to this approach is that it might increase the monopoly power of the energy industry.

To the extent that the pricing policies of firms fail to take account of the costs to society of health damages and property losses resulting from pollution, private industry will invest too little in research and development to reduce pollution from fossil fuels or to develop clean sources of energy. John Tilton believes the best way government can induce private companies to address environmental concerns is by a tax system:

> The solution most economists advocate for this problem involves government charges or taxes on polluters equivalent to the pollution costs of their activities. Internalizing pollution costs would correct the distortion in private incentives against environmental R&D. The U.S. government, however, has not adopted this procedure, but has opted instead for a system of regulations that allows firms to pollute up to a point without any charge and then enjoins further

pollution at any price. Among other inefficiencies, this procedure distorts R&D incentives. Firms whose activities are not constrained by the regulations will carry out too little environmental R&D, those seriously affected may carry out too much.[15]

Another reason the private sector may not make adequate investments in energy research and development is the present double taxation of corporate profits. Corporations must pay a 48 percent federal corporate income tax on profits above a certain level; when added to the personal taxes paid by shareholders on dividends received, this reduces incentives to invest in corporate research and development projects. Allowing firms to deduct their research and development expenditures from corporate income before computing taxes offsets only a part of the disincentive to invest in R&D. In other words, since a company's gains from research and development are taxed, expenditures for such programs will be reduced. Government could further increase private energy firms' incentives by reducing corporate tax rates.

Although our discussion so far has focused on private industry's contributions to energy research and development, this is not to say that all such activities are currently in private hands. Table 3-5 shows the estimated expenditures on energy research and development for 1963 and 1973 by both the private and the public sectors. In 1963 the federal government spent relatively little on research and development of petro-

Table 3-5
Estimated Private and Public Expenditures on Energy Research and Development, 1963 and 1973
(millions of dollars)

Sector	1963			1973		
	Private	Public	Total	Private	Public	Total
Petroleum and natural gas	469	56	525	600	26	626
All electricity	371	385	756	300	421	721
Nuclear fission	—	293	—	—	356	—
Nuclear fusion	—	36	—	—	65	—
Other electric	—	56	—	—	—a	—
All other	17	19	36	100	180	280
Coal	—	15	—	—	94	—
Environment	—	—	—	—	55	—
Other	—	4	—	—	31	—
Total	857	460	1317	1000	627	1627

— Zero or negligible.

aExpenditures in this category were included under the "all other" categories.

Note: The 1963 expenditures are inflated by the implicit price deflator for the gross national product so that all expenditures in this table are expressed in constant 1973 dollars.

Source: John E. Tilton, *U.S. Energy R&D Policy: The Role of Economics* (Baltimore, Md.: Johns Hopkins University Press, 1974), pp. 11, 14.

leum, natural gas, coal, or environmental protection. By 1973 the federal government had increased its research and development expenditures on coal and the environment, but it had decreased its relatively small expenditures on petroleum and natural gas.

Before the oil embargo in 1973 over two-thirds of federal funding of research and development funding was going toward nuclear power. This is reasonable, since expanded federal activities in traditional energy areas would be likely to supplant or duplicate research and development already being carried out by the private sector. (Private firms of course have an incentive to try to have the federal government pay for research and development programs they would have conducted themselves in any event.) By 1977 federal expenditures on energy research and development had reached 3.2 billion dollars. This was equivalent to 2.4 billion dollars in 1973 constant prices—nearly four times the level of expenditures in 1973, before the oil embargo.[16]

Exclusive federal control of all research and development activities to develop energy resources could eliminate duplication of effort both between the private and federal sectors and within the private sector. The federal government could screen all proposed projects and approve or issue permits to those projects that meet certain criteria.

Eliminating duplication is not, however, always a wise strategy. The chances for technical and economic success are improved by duplication; that is, not only does duplication make it more likely that a solution to a given problem will be found, but when two different processes are developed to meet the same goal, often a combination of the two proves cheaper or more efficient than either one.

Federal control of energy research and development also might have negative effects on private firms' incentives for doing research and development, as John Tilton notes:

> The ability to get R&D contracts and to please government sponsors becomes important. This tends to shift the emphasis from achieving commercially useful and profitable results to producing difficult and impressive technical advances that may or may not be of great use to society. Even more important, the incentives to produce any results are diminished because a large part of the cost of failure is borne by the government. In addition, a large portion of the benefits of success are inappropriable since the right to patent or withhold information on new developments produced under government contracts is limited.[17]

The ultimate reason for engaging in research and development is to find new techniques for producing energy that are economically competitive with existing technologies and fuel sources. Exclusive federal government control of research and development on energy resources might introduce rigidity into the process with the result that some potentially promising projects would be ignored in favor of fulfilling contract commitments to earlier projects, even though they have become unpromising as research has progressed. The private enterprise system has incentives to abandon projects that will not produce commercially useful results and to minimize losses from false starts. Government-funded projects would more likely be completed even if the outcomes are of no value, since private funds are not at stake. It also might be argued that it has been the drive of individual citizens and businesses to build a better mousetrap that has led to most technological advances in this country. In addition, technological progress might be slower if the federal government assumes exclusive control of energy research and development.

Public Safety and the Environment

Public safety and environmental quality are often cited as two areas where private enterprises fail to make adequate investments to protect society's welfare. Air pollution from burning fossil fuels, thermal pollution of lakes and streams by nuclear power plants, strip mining of western coal reserves, oil spills from tankers and offshore drilling, threats to public safety in transporting liquefied natural gas, and risks of sabotage of nuclear power plants or proliferation of nuclear weapons have been mentioned as reasons the federal government should take control of the development of energy resources.

If the costs of developing and implementing methods of preventing pollution could be passed on to the consumer in the form of higher prices for energy, then, say economists, private enterprises would have the incentive to invest in the socially optimal amount of pollution control. Public knowledge about the costs of dealing with pollution is limited, however, and the idea of using price changes or taxes instead of fines is not widely accepted as a way of reducing pollution and offsetting such costs.

In many cases the costs of pollution may be relatively small, and in others such costs may in fact be properly reflected in the market price of the energy resource. If coal companies strip mine coal deposits and alter the terrain on property they own, then they will bear the costs of the lowered property values and will excavate

38

only on property where the value of the coal is great enough to cover both the excavation costs and the loss in property value. They also will willingly restore the property after excavation if the resulting increase in property values exceeds the costs of reclamation. To the extent that strip mining imposes costs on neighboring parties, individual states may levy taxes or pass regulations on strip mining and energy development where the potential damages warrant it. Uniform national strip-mining legislation supported by the Carter administration would eliminate this flexibility.

The outer continental shelf is a promising source of oil and natural gas; drilling there could reduce somewhat this country's dependence on foreign oil. Progress in undertaking to drill for these offshore resources has been slowed by several problems: fears of environmental damage, the federal government's hesitance to lease offshore drilling rights, and price controls on domestic oil and natural gas which have reduced producers' incentives. Drilling for offshore oil presents less danger of oil spills than does transporting oil from the Middle East. Environmental damages actually might be reduced by increased production in the continental shelf. As Charles Matthews has put it:

> The recent report on petroleum and marine environment published by the National Academy of Sciences estimated that 6.1 million metric tons of petroleum hydrocarbons enter the oceans annually. More than one-third of that amount is from transportation, which takes into account tankers, drydocks, terminal operations, buildings, and accidents. The contribution of offshore oil production was estimated at only one-twenty-sixth of the amount put in by transportation. Natural seeps—or God's pollution or nature's pollution, whatever one wants to call it—put into the oceans eight times the amount of pollution that is put there by offshore production.[18]

Looking at this issue another way, it could be said that by encouraging oil and natural gas production abroad, we are in effect shifting much environmental pollution away from the United States onto other countries and parts of the world—where, indeed, there is less care to avoid it or effort to remedy it than there is here.

Federal control of the development of energy resources has been most extensive in the nuclear power industry. The level of future federal involvement is likely to depend on whether continued development of the liquid metal fast breeder reactor is undertaken, and whether private firms will be allowed to produce enriched uranium to fuel domestic and foreign nuclear power plants. Many nations already have nuclear power programs and many more are planning them. As the Committee on Economic Development has pointed out, however, "Nuclear energy almost certainly will be essential to meeting the world's future energy needs, but its weapon potential is a threat to the very existence of all nations."[19] If other countries or the United States develop the capacity to retrieve plutonium by reprocessing spent reactor fuel without adequate safety precautions, then the possibility exists that terrorists or nation states could use the plutonium to construct nuclear weapons.

An unresolved issue of nuclear policy is the proper role of the U.S. government in the ownership or control of production facilities for nuclear fuel. All uranium enrichment in the United States is now done by the federal government, using facilities originally built for weapons programs. Further development of uranium enrichment will be for power reactors; therefore, from now on, the major use of the enrichment facilities originally designed for the production of weapons-grade uranium will be production of reactor fuel.

The key point for the United States is that there is an essential diplomatic role for the federal government parallel to an essential production and commercial role for private enterprise. Coordinating these two roles is an immediate challenge.[20]

Whether to proceed with the development of the liquid metal fast breeder reactor, which would produce more plutonium for fuel than it uses, has been widely debated. Table 3-6 shows actual and projected annual expenditures on the fast breeder reactor. President Carter and others have opposed further development of the Clinch River liquid metal fast breeder reactor demonstration plant on the grounds of the threat of nuclear proliferation, high costs, and the possibility of the plant's obsolescence as other new technologies, such as fusion reactors, have begun to show promise. The majority of the members of Congress have so far favored continuing the project, and preliminary analysis has been conducted of the prospects for adapting the reactor to commercial use in the private sector.[21]

Superseding State and Local Authority

Regulation of electric and natural gas utilities by state and local regulatory commissions has often resulted in price structures that have led to misallocation of scarce energy resources and have violated accepted principles of energy conservation. President Carter's National Energy Plan proposes thorough reform of electricity pricing.

Table 3-6
Expenditures on the Liquid Metal Fast Breeder Reactor Program, 1947–1979
(millions of dollars)

Fiscal Year	Annual Expenditure	Cumulative Expenditures
1947	0.9	0.9
1948	0.6	1.5
1949	1.1	2.6
1950	2.4	5.0
1951	0.7	5.7
1952	3.5	9.2
1953	3.4	12.6
1954	3.9	16.5
1955	5.0	21.5
1956	5.8	27.3
1957	7.6	34.9
1958	16.1	51.0
1959	21.8	72.8
1960	20.3	93.1
1961	14.3	107.4
1962	17.1	124.5
1963	26.0	150.5
1964	26.7	177.2
1965	34.1	211.3
1966	42.6	253.9
1967	78.0	331.9
1968	95.0	426.9
1969	106.0	532.9
1970	120.0	652.9
1971	176.0	828.9
1972	205.0	1,033.9
1973	253.8	1,287.7
1974	356.8[a]	1,644.5
1975	477.0[b]	2,121.5
1976	538.6[b]	2,660.1
1977	510.8[b]	3,170.9
1978	524.2[b]	3,695.1
1979	506.0[b]	4,201.1

[a]Planned.

[b]Recommended.

Source: Brian G. Chow, *The Liquid Metal Fast Breeder Reactor: An Economic Analysis* (Washington, D.C.: American Enterprise Institute, 1975), p. 13.

Electrical energy is difficult and expensive to store, so a utility's need for plant and equipment is determined by its peak demand. If electricity consumption during peak periods were reduced, fewer costly new additions to utility capacity would be needed. Equally important, since peaking units commonly burn oil and gas, a reduction in peak demand would save these scarce fuels.

Accordingly, comprehensive utility reform legislation is proposed. State public utility commissions would require their regulated utilities to reform rate structures in the interest of conservation and equity.

Such reform would be a prerequisite to future rate increases. The program includes the following elements:

—Electric utilities would be required to phase out declining block, and other rates that do not reflect costs; gas utilities would also be required to phase out declining block rates.

—Electric utilities would be required to offer either daily off-peak rates to each customer who is willing to pay metering costs, or provide a direct load management system. Off-peak rates would provide a strong incentive for customers, particularly industrial customers, to shift energy use from peak to off-peak periods. Similarly, homeowners would have an incentive to wash dishes and clothes at night when rates were lower, or to install equipment that stores energy during off-peak hours for use during peak hours.

—Electric utilities would be required to offer lower rates to customers who are willing to have their power interrupted at times of highest peak demand.

—Master metering—the use of a single meter for multi-unit buildings or complexes—would generally be prohibited in new structures. Individual metering induces energy conservation, in some cases as much as 30 percent.

—Electric utilities would be prohibited from discriminating against solar and other renewable energy sources.[22]

To some extent the need for these reforms may already have passed, since a large number of utilities and state regulatory commissions have taken these steps on their own. Another objection to such a proposal is that federal imposition of regulations on state agencies takes away the states' right to determine their own regulations according to their individual needs and unique circumstances. States would not be allowed to set up rate structures favoring industrial users to try to attract more businesses to their communities, or to set rates favoring the poor, without federal permission. Before the federal government tries to reform the states it should first reform itself, it is sometimes argued, by eliminating the subsidies—such as those granted by the Rural Electrification Administration—that encourage energy consumption.

Exclusive control of the development of energy resources by the federal government might conflict with the rights of states to prevent the despoilment of their environments. As Governor Michael Dukakis of Massachusetts has noted, ''Only a few states are blessed with an abundant natural supply of energy resources.

Some 65 percent of this country's oil and gas is produced in just three states. Most of our uranium is found in two states, and most of our coal is taken from five. All told, fully 60 percent of America's energy supplies can be found in just seven states."[23] Federal control of the rate at which energy resources are extracted and of the precautions taken to prevent despoilment of the environment could result in greater despoilment than some states would otherwise have allowed because of pressures from states that have neither energy reserves nor the pollution problems extraction creates. Other states might desire to develop their resources at a faster rate than federal controls allowed.

Equalizing the Distribution of Energy Resources

The prices of most goods and services in the United States are determined by forces of supply and demand with no government intervention. Firms are free to decide how much to produce and offer for sale, and consumers are free to buy whatever quantities they desire. If a resource becomes scarcer, as oil did in 1973 when the Arabs began restricting supplies, its price rises until consumers cut back on the quantities purchased and producers put additional supplies on the market, thus bringing supply and demand again in equilibrium. Sugar, coffee, and oranges are examples of food items that temporarily became scarce in recent years so that their prices rose.

Many people believe, however, that unregulated energy prices would have undesirable effects on the distribution of income in the United States. They argue that because the demand for energy is universal and always high, free market prices would place an unfair burden on consumers—and especially on the poor who would have limited access to energy as prices rose—and provide unjustified benefits for the rich.

The federal government has been actively involved in controlling natural gas and oil prices since the 1950s. Since a 1954 Supreme Court decision clarifying its authority to regulate prices, the Federal Power Commission (now the Federal Energy Regulatory Commission) has controlled the wellhead price of natural gas flowing in interstate commerce. As a result of these price controls, according to the National Energy Plan, in 1976

> natural gas in the interstate market sold at wellhead rates that were 25 percent of the Btu equivalent price of imported crude oil. The Natural Gas Act never contemplated the dramatic increase in demand for natural gas which has resulted from the sudden quadrupling of the world price of oil in 1973–74 and from growing environmental concern in recent years. As a result of regulation under that act, natural gas is now substantially underpriced, and there is excess demand.[24]

The price controls on interstate natural gas differentially affect the welfare of several groups of Americans. Customers in the interstate market benefit from being able to buy gas at only a fraction of its intrastate cost, which is not controlled. But they bear greater risks of supply interruptions (such as those that occurred in the Midwest during the unusually harsh winter of 1976–1977). Interstate inventories are subject to depletion because of high consumption, reduced exploration incentives, and producers' inclination to sell as much of their supply as possible at the higher intrastate price. Potential customers who would like to use natural gas even at unregulated prices, but who are unable to obtain it because of rationing, are inconvenienced by the price controls. Families desiring to build a new home with gas heating may have to use a more expensive system or postpone their purchase until gas hookups become available. Industries desiring to use natural gas, but unable to purchase it at controlled prices, are forced either to abandon production plans or to move to natural-gas-producing states where prices are not controlled. The regional inequities caused by the interstate price controls include an increase in employment in the sun belt states which comes at the expense of the loss of employment opportunities in the Northeast. All Americans suffer to the extent that artificially low prices encourage waste and overuse of scarce energy resources.

From 1959 until 1971 the federal government imposed mandatory oil import quotas to restrict petroleum supplies from abroad. The result was that the domestic crude oil price was about $1.25 per barrel above the price of imported oil.[25] The main burden of these higher prices fell on regions such as New England, which, being far from the domestic oil-producing regions, would have found it cheaper to rely more on imports. The major beneficiaries of the import quotas were the owners of domestic oil reserves.

In 1971 the Nixon administration instituted price controls on crude oil and certain other products. While the other products have since been decontrolled, domestic oil has not. By setting domestic prices below world oil prices, the federal government has discouraged domestic production, which declined from a peak of about 10 million barrels per day in 1970 to about 8 million barrels per day in 1977.[26] By averaging in controlled domestic crude oil prices with higher imported prices to set the consumer price, the federal government encourages overconsumption of oil, gasoline, and oil products, creating a demand that must be met by imports. Since most of the price paid for oil imports from the Middle East represents monopoly profits to the OPEC cartel members, the federal pricing policy causes the United States to spend billions of dollars subsidizing foreign oil-producing states in order to deny domestic producers windfall profits. In the words of Melvin Laird, "The effect of this pricing policy . . . has been to place us in the anomalous position of paying foreign producers more for a product than we are willing to pay domestic producers."[27]

President Carter's proposed National Energy Plan would eliminate part of the subsidy to foreign nations by charging consumers world prices for domestic and foreign crude oil. The government would do this, however, not by decontrolling domestic prices but by introducing a set of taxes on various categories of domestic oil production. For example, taxes would be levied equal to the difference between world prices and 1977 price ceilings of $5.25 per barrel for old oil and $11.28 per barrel for new oil (adjusted for inflation). Oil newly discovered after April 20, 1977, would be taxed at a rate equal to the difference between world oil prices and the 1977 world price of $13.50 per barrel (adjusted for inflation).[28] Because the prices received by domestic producers still would be held below the world price of oil, incentives for domestic production would continue to be limited and oil imports encouraged, though not to the same extent they are at present.

A major concern of federal policy makers has been that owners of oil and natural gas firms should not receive windfall profits as a result of higher world oil prices. The President's National Energy Plan states, "Total deregulation would result in a massive transfer of income from the American public to the oil and gas producers, amounting to $14 to $15 billion, nearly 1 percent of the U.S. gross national product."[29] These windfall profits to the oil and gas producers would most likely be invested either in further development of energy resources or in other nonenergy related projects, or be passed on to the stockholders (most of whom are American citizens) in the form of dividends or capital gains on their stock holdings. A large proportion of the profits would go to the government through federal and state corporate taxes and personal income tax payments.

If we agree that it is socially beneficial to reverse the decline in the real incomes and welfare of the poor resulting from increased oil and natural gas prices since 1973, there are more efficient means to achieve this goal than price controls. Price controls benefit all consumers who are able to make purchases from available supplies, but especially the rich. Since higher-income families purchase larger amounts of oil and natural gas, they benefit more from the controlled price savings. Poor families may even be injured if price controls limit their ability to obtain gas supplies and cause them to turn to higher-priced alternative fuels and energy products. Rationing, which is yet another alternative, is generally considered to be unpopular and not suited for American political and social institutions in peacetime. Numerous other means are available to compensate for inequities in income distribution besides price controls and rationing, however. Increased welfare and social security payments or government rebates are direct alternatives to introducing distortions into the energy market and, among other things, subsidizing the heating costs of the wealthy. Melvin Laird has summed up the problem:

The problems of the poor in paying for increased energy costs is a highly emotional and difficult one. Because our society is still ordered in large measure in reliance on technology and living patterns developed during a period of much lower energy costs, near-term adjustment to higher prices will be especially difficult. Single family dwellings require heat and electricity, and there is clearly a minimum beyond which even ardent conservation cannot cut without leading to a standard of living which we as a society have judged unbearably difficult. The wide dispersal of housing and the separation of housing from jobs, coupled with the lack of adequate mass transportation in many areas, mean for at least the near term continued reliance on individual transportation in automobiles. However, price increases in any product are always painful, and much more so for those used as pervasively as energy. Yet energy is not unique in its necessity to everyday life. Food supplies certainly fall in that category even more dramatically. We have not, however, radically changed our food pricing to accommodate the poor but rather have designed particular social welfare programs for the poor. The problem then is not to require an energy policy to cure the social problems of the country but rather to recognize the social impact of a correct energy policy and then to make a welfare or subsidy system equitable in avoiding untoward hardship.[30]

The United States economy is a dynamic and diverse one. People frequently move, change jobs, and invent new products or improve old ones. Americans produce innumerable goods and services to reflect the varied likes and dislikes of the people. The complexity involved in planning the development and distribution of resources in even one sector of the economy is immense. That it is feasible has been demonstrated in the Soviet Union and other Communist countries.

The costs to the public of expanding the government sector to administer federal regulation of the energy industry need to be weighed against the benefits. Murray L. Weidenbaum asserts that the direct costs of government regulators to taxpayers in fiscal 1978 reached $3.8 billion and that "professional studies show that the annual [indirect] cost to the consumer of excessive federal government regulation comes to over $60 billion a year."[31] Whether the costs of decreased individual freedom available in a private economy are surpassed by the benefits of exclusive federal control of energy development and distribution is subject to dispute. The answer depends on the relative strengths and weaknesses of government and business in developing and distributing energy in an efficient, socially beneficial manner.

NOTES

[1] *Webster's Seventh New Collegiate Dictionary* (Springfield, Mass.: G. & C. Merriam Co., 1977), p. 182.

[2] George Leland Bach, *Macroeconomics: Analysis and Applications* (Englewood Cliffs, N.J.: Prentice-Hall, Inc., 1977), p. 347.

[3] U.S., Executive Office of the President, *The National Energy Plan* (Washington, D.C., 1977), p. 33.

[4] Ibid., p. 26.

[5] Ford Foundation Energy Policy Project, *A Time to Choose: America's Energy Future* (Cambridge, Mass.: Ballinger Publishing Co., 1974), p. 231.

[6] U.S., Congress, House Committee on the Judiciary, Subcommittee on Monopolies and Commercial Law, *Energy Industry Investigation,* 94th Cong., 1st and 2nd sess., 1976, p. 299.

[7] *Wall Street Journal,* April 7, 1978, p. 1.

[8] Edward J. Mitchell, ed., *Vertical Integration in the Oil Industry* (Washington, D.C.: American Enterprise Institute, 1976), p. 45.

[9] Ibid., p. 47.

[10] "The New Oil Game: Diversification," *Business Week,* April 24, 1978, p. 77.

[11] According to statistics compiled by Citibank of New York.

[12] Executive Office, *National Energy Plan,* p. 20.

[13] Walter S. Mossberg, "Carter Starts on Second Energy Proposal, Though His First Is Still before Congress," *Wall Street Journal,* April 11, 1978, p. 3.

[14] John E. Tilton, *U.S. Energy R&D Policy: The Role of Economics* (Washington, D.C.: Resources for the Future, Inc., 1974), p. 29.

[15] Ibid., p. 32.

[16] U.S., Executive Office of the President, Office of Management and Budget, *Special Analyses: Budget of the United States Government, Fiscal Year 1979,* p. 312.

[17] Tilton, *U.S. Energy R&D,* p. 46.

[18] Charles Matthews, in *The Question of Offshore Oil,* ed. Edward J. Mitchell (Washington, D.C.: American Enterprise Institute, 1976), pp. 52–53.

[19] Committee for Economic Development, *Nuclear Energy and National Security* (New York, 1972), p. 12.

[20] Ibid., pp. 24–25.

[21] U.S., General Accounting Office, *Considerations for Commercializing the Liquid Metal Fast Breeder Reactor* (Washington, D.C., 1976).

[22] Executive Office, *National Energy Plan,* p. 46.

[23] Michael Dukakis, "Introduction," in *Energy: Regional Goals and the National Interest,* ed. Edward J. Mitchell (Washington, D.C.: American Enterprise Institute, 1976), p. 3.

[24] Executive Office, *National Energy Plan,* pp. 18, 52.

[25] Walter J. Mead, *An Economic Appraisal of President Carter's Energy Program,* Reprint Paper 7 (Los Angeles: International Institute for Economic Research, 1977), p. 8.

[26] Ibid.

[27] Melvin R. Laird, *Energy—A Crisis in Public Policy* (Washington, D.C.: American Enterprise Institute, 1977), p. 6.

[28] Executive Office, *National Energy Plan,* pp. 50–51.

[29] Ibid., p. 51.

[30] Laird, *Energy—A Crisis in Public Policy,* pp. 7–8.

[31] Murray L. Weidenbaum, "A Free Market Approach to Economic Policy," *Challenge,* March–April, 1978, p. 41.

Chapter 4

ENERGY CONSERVATION

*Resolved: That the federal government should establish
a comprehensive program to significantly reduce energy consumption
in the United States.*

The second debate resolution presents some problems of interpretation. *The federal government* may again be defined as in chapter 3, and a *comprehensive program* should be taken to mean one that attempts to take into consideration all energy uses and avoids self-defeating or contradictory measures. However, a number of interpretations might conceivably be placed on the phrase *significantly reduce energy consumption*. Taken literally, it calls for a reduction in the amount of energy consumed each year in the United States. Energy consumption could be defined in terms of Btu equivalents, or in terms of the amount of money spent on it, or perhaps in other ways. The task of the affirmative would then be to argue that this figure should be reduced by some "significant" amount, perhaps as little as 2 or 5 percent. This interpretation, however, is a difficult one to sustain in discussion, largely because most authorities on the subject view even reducing the rate of growth of energy use to zero as a difficult and probably burdensome goal.

A second interpretation of the resolution might be that energy consumption per capita (or energy consumption per real dollar of GNP) should be reduced. Such an interpretation is more common in calls for energy conservation. Here too, however, population growth and growth in real income make absolute declines in total U.S. energy consumption unlikely, as we shall see.

A third possible interpretation of the resolution is that it calls for a reduction in the rate of growth of energy use. This might, in its practical aspects, be very similar to reducing per capita energy consumption, but it focuses on a different set of numbers.

Overview of the Issues

Several arguments can be made in favor of reducing energy consumption. If the United States used less oil, gas, and coal each year, more reserves would remain in the ground for future use. Since these resources are limited in amount, it obviously would not be good policy to use them all over the next five years; but neither would it make sense to be excessively sparing in their use (to the point, let us say, of cutting yearly consumption by 90 percent). To justify cutting back, one would have to show that present consumption of these resources is too great, and that it will prevent future generations from getting their share of energy resources.

Another justification for reducing consumption lies in the actual and potential effects on the environment of heavy energy use. One might argue that it would be a wiser use of resources if we cut back use of fossil fuels and of nuclear energy in order to limit their adverse effects on other natural resources. Demonstrating this would require summoning evidence that damage and hazards to the environment are better reduced in this fashion than through other measures.

One could, of course, argue that less energy consumption is good for its own sake, technology having advanced to the point where increases in material well-being decrease human happiness. Such a position, whatever its merits, probably would take one beyond the prosaic limits of most discussion about energy policy.

Another justification, covered at greater length in the next chapter, is that decreased consumption would allow the United States to rely to a greater degree on its own energy resources than it does at present. Reductions in energy consumption, if aimed at this objective, would be geared toward curbing imports.

Those who advocate a reduction of energy consumption might base their case on (1) the specific aim (conserving resources above what would otherwise take place or working toward energy independence); (2) the argument that reducing energy consumption is the best way to achieve that aim; and (3) the argument that a comprehensive federal program is the best means to achieve a reduction of energy consumption. Rebutting the resolution would entail countering each of these arguments.

How Can Energy Consumption Be Reduced?
Any of a number of policy options might be used to try to reduce energy consumption. Which approach one prefers depends in large part on how responsive to economic incentives one believes energy use by consumers and industry to be. An optimistic view on the matter could lead one to espouse a system of taxes on the use of fossil fuels and nuclear energy, and subsidies for installing insulation and other devices that reduce energy use. If one judges that such incentives would not bring about the desired reductions, however, other measures are at hand. Quotas, tariffs, rationing, reduction of speed limits, nationwide revision of building codes, appliance efficiency standards, and other energy conservation policies might be introduced. Adopting a hard line on oil imports, nuclear reactor construction, dam siting, strip mining, and offshore and shale oil development might also be a way to compel a reduction in energy consumption.

One objection that might be raised against a policy of incentives (taxes on fossil fuels, for example) is that energy is not the only resource worth conserving. Discouraging energy use may encourage greater use of other scarce resources, such as those used to make insulation. Economists in particular argue that if consumers pay the true social cost for the resources they use, efficiency in resource use will result automatically.

Similarly, a possible objection to an array of prohibitions and restrictions is that such measures inhibit people's freedom to choose how best to employ the resources available to them. If the prices of fuels reflect their true resource value to society, then their use should not be further encouraged or discouraged. It is argued that people themselves are the best judges of how to use something in scarce supply (again, when it is correctly priced). Any attempt to determine the most socially beneficial way of using energy by means of regulations about home insulation, what appliances may be sold, and which fuel may be used for various purposes is bound to be complex and likely to promote inefficiencies in consumption and production.

Energy Use in the Future. The federal government and a number of independent organizations and researchers have made predictions about the use of energy in future years. While such predictions are necessary and useful, it is also true that prediction is sometimes called "the fool's art." Many predictions have been made in the past about energy use, and it may help us in assessing those being made now to look first at some predecessors. As mentioned in chapter 2, a number of authorities predicted at various times over the last hundred years that the United States would run out of oil in only a few years. More recently, Lawrence Rocks and Richard P. Runyon, authors of *The Energy Crisis* (published in 1972), included an appendix in their book entitled "Timetable for an Energy Crisis." Presumably they intended their timetable as a prediction of what would happen if American energy policy continued to be as indecisive as it had been so far. "The thesis of this book is that the most profound issue we face today is an impending power shortage." They conclude that "restrictions upon future rates of energy consumption are inescapable."[1] Their predictions to 1980, made at the beginning of this decade, are presented in table 4-1 and testify to the hazards of soothsaying.

Another way to consider predictions is to compare different predictions about energy consumption for a given year in the future. Table 4-2 has four projections made between 1963 and 1974. Such figures can vary widely: two government predictions made within two years of each other, by the Department of the Interior and Project Independence, differ on the order of 33 to 63 percent concerning energy use in the year 2000. But all studies anticipated increased energy use. The lower estimates from Project Independence show use ex-

---

Table 4-1
Timetable for an Energy Crisis, 1972

Restrictions on Energy Consumption	Effective Date
Curtailed heating (and air conditioning) in shopping centers, department stores, theaters, and restaurants	Early 1970s
Curtailed heating (and air conditioning) in public buildings, schools, houses, and hospitals	Late 1970s
Gasoline rationing for everyone: no pleasure driving, car pools, increased public transportation	Late 1970s if we are obliged to supply Japan and Europe; otherwise, by the 1980s
Government control of key industries by rationing energy	End of the 1970s
Government spending of hundreds of billions of dollars in crash programs for energy procurement	End of the 1970s

Source: Lawrence Rocks and Richard P. Runyon, *The Energy Crisis* (New York: Crown Publishers, 1972), p. 176.

Table 4-2
Projected Energy Use for the United States
(quadrillion Btu)

Study and Year	Projected Energy Use	
	1980	2000
Landsberg (1963)[a]	79.2	135.2
Darmstadter (1971)[b]	95.1	190.0
Department of Interior (1972)[c]	—[e]	172–192
Project Independence (1974)[d]	86.0–91.4	117.7–129.2

[a]Hans H. Landsberg, Leonard L. Fischman, and Joseph L. Fisher, *Resources in America's Future* (Baltimore, Md.: Johns Hopkins University Press, 1963), p. 290.

[b]Joel Darmstadter, "Energy Consumption: Trends and Patterns," in *Energy, Economic Growth and the Environment,* ed. Sam H. Schurr (Baltimore, Md.: Johns Hopkins University Press, 1972).

[c]Reported in U.S., Congress, Senate, Committee on Interior and Insular Affairs, *Readings on Energy Conservation,* 94th Cong., 1st sess., 1975, p. 247.

[d]Reported in U.S., Congress, House, Committee on Interstate and Foreign Commerce, *Basic Energy Data,* 94th Cong., 1st sess., 1975, p. 102.

[e]No prediction made.

pected "with conservation," yet it still is anticipated to increase by 36 percent between 1980 and 2000.

The Ford Foundation Energy Policy Project

A study that has set the tone for much of the policy debate in the 1970s is the final report issued by the Ford Foundation's Energy Policy Project, *A Time to Choose: America's Energy Future.* Because the keynote of the report was that success in energy policy depends on conservation, it seems appropriate to include a review of its findings and of some of the criticisms the report evoked.

Review of the Project's Findings. The fundamental policy recommendation of the report rested on the finding that conservation of energy is a way to reduce some of the undesirable consequences of energy use.

It is this Project's conclusion that the size and shape of most energy problems are determined in large part by how fast energy consumption grows. Some problems, of course, such as high prices and their impact on the poor, must be faced whatever the policy adopted on conservation. But slower growth makes many energy-related problems less formidable.

It is, of course, a mistake to regard energy conservation as an end in itself; that puts the cart before the horse. Conservation is worthwhile as a means to

alleviate shortages, preserve the environment, stretch out the supply of finite resources and protect the independence of U.S. foreign policy.[2]

To demonstrate how less energy might be used in an effort to lessen the unfavorable consequences mentioned, the report presents three "scenarios" of future energy use in the United States (see table 4-3). Under the Historical Growth scenario, energy use (defined in terms of Btu) continues to grow at the rate it did from 1950 to 1970, that is, at 3.4 percent per year. The report concedes that since energy prices fell during those years, it would be unrealistic to expect such a growth rate to continue unless subsidies to energy consumption are provided.

The second possibility is the Technical Fix scenario, which envisages a 1.9 percent rate of growth, and which, the report contends, "can provide essentially the same level of energy services (miles of travel, quality of housing and levels of heating and cooling, manufacturing output) as the Historical Growth scenario. What is required is that the nation adopt specific energy saving technologies, such as better insulation and better auto fuel economy, to perform these functions."[3] The mix of policies that would underlie such a slower growth in energy use includes changes in electrical utility rates, upgrading local building codes, technical assistance to the building trades, changes in automobile design, fuel economy regulations, more efficient industrial processes, and more centralized industrial planning to take advantage of the possibility of using the steam that results from certain industrial processes to generate electricity.[4]

The third proposal is a Zero Energy Growth scenario, in which *increases* in energy consumption are reduced to zero by the year 2000. The justifications for considering such a proposal are that it would

- limit industrialization of areas that have hitherto remained undeveloped

Table 4-3
Energy Growth under Alternative Scenarios
(quadrillion Btu)

Year	Scenario		
	Historical Growth	Technical Fix	Zero Energy Growth
1973	75.0	75.0	75.0
1985	116.1	91.3	88.1
2000	186.7	124.0	100.0

Source: Compiled from Ford Foundation Energy Policy Project, *A Time to Choose: America's Energy Future* (Cambridge, Mass.: Ballinger Publishing Co., 1974), tables 1, 5, and 16.

- reduce pollution from fossil fuels at less cost than other methods
- avoid nuclear accidents and other potentially serious consequences of energy use
- make it easier for developing nations to grow by reducing the United States' share of world energy consumption
- allow the development of decentralized energy sources not dominated by growth-oriented bureaucracies
- bring about a change in social attitudes and values, shifting emphasis from material goods to non-material needs, especially at a time when some people believe that we have reached the "saturation" level of material goods.[5]

Clearly, the Zero Energy Growth (ZEG) scenario corresponds most closely to the policy set forth in the narrow interpretation of the debate resolution presented at the beginning of this chapter. ZEG would imply, if not a reduction in energy consumption, at least a reduction in per capita consumption, as well as a decrease in the ratio of energy use to GNP. (These latter two implications of course depend on continued increases in population and GNP.)

The specific policies which the report's authors say would allow the United States to level off in energy use by the year 2000 include an energy sales tax; increased benefits to the poor to offset the effects of that tax (more public transportation, health care, housing, clean streets and parks, education, and nursing homes and other old-age benefits, for example); either a heavy tax on automobiles that get low gasoline mileage or enforced mileage standards; and stricter building codes. Other policies that would contribute to ZEG include research and development efforts in energy conservation, upgrading rail services, expanding urban mass transit systems, and developing a system of bikeways.[6]

"The major finding from our work," conclude the authors, "is that it is desirable, technically feasible, and economical to reduce the rate of energy growth in the years ahead, at least to the levels of a long-term average of about 2 percent annually."[7] Such a policy aim, they contend, can be realized without affecting the rate of growth of GNP. The Technical Fix scenario (which corresponds to a 2 percent rate of energy growth) is possible, they say, by saving energy in three areas:

- Buildings can be constructed and operated so as to reduce energy requirements for heating and cooling.

- Gasoline mileage for automobiles can be increased.
- Industrial processes can be redesigned so that heat now wasted is used to generate electricity and for other useful purposes.[8]

The Response to the Energy Policy Project. Following its publication in 1974, *A Time to Choose* provoked replies from several quarters. The Institute for Contemporary Studies, for example, asked ten authorities on energy matters, seven of them economists, to comment on the report; their comments were collected in a volume entitled *No Time to Confuse,* issued in 1975. Thomas Gale Moore, director of research at the Hoover Institution for War, Revolution, and Peace, summarized a large share of the criticism: "The entire report reflects an assumption that it is desirable to reduce energy use above and beyond whatever reduction simple market forces would produce. The rationale for this belief is not clear."[9] Focusing on more specific issues, Moore writes:

The report . . . recommend[s] all sorts of mandatory measures to reduce energy consumption, such as federally imposed minimum fuel economy performance standards for automobiles, a federal loan program to provide credit for energy saving investment, and new minimum standards of insulation for buildings. But if these steps are as economically efficient as the authors believe, consumers, builders, and auto buyers will require them without federal coercion.[10]

George Hilton, professor of economics at the University of California, Los Angeles, offers a similar criticism. The contention in *A Time to Choose* that reduced energy use will have little future economic cost is correct, according to Hilton, "only if the authors are right in their presumption that the market has neglected a large number of opportunities for improvement in energy use."[11] For example, the authors of *A Time to Choose* argued that houses currently being built are not energy efficient because home buyers tend to ignore operating costs entailed in fuel expenditures. Economist Armen Alchian responds to this by asking rhetorically, "What is the evidence? Are houses in the cold Northeast built the same as in Florida or California?" He argues that regional differences in construction indicate that buyers and builders are aware that the efficient use of all resources means that not only energy but other resources as well must not be overused.[12]

Yet another criticism of the Ford Foundation study's endorsement of conservation is that conservation would not, as claimed, be "the most effective unilateral action that nation can take"[13] with respect to the international energy situation. Morris Adelman contends that conservation measures in the United States would in fact bolster the OPEC cartel:

> The truth is that in a monopolized market, energy conservation by customers is a good way to force up the price . . . The more drastic the conservation of U.S. supply, the less elastic our demand. People who are induced by education or other non-price methods to reduce their house temperatures will not be as responsive to higher prices at 66° as they were at 72°. . . . Hence, a rational monopolist will raise prices knowing that he has lost some of the market anyway, because under the new conditions consumers will not reduce usage as much as they would have previously.[14]

Not all criticism of the report fell one way, however. Dean E. Abrahamson of the Ford Foundation Energy Policy Project Advisory Board was, although in general agreement with the report, critical of its "timid" stance on some subjects:

> The suggestion that zero energy growth . . . is an extreme case is ludicrous . . . Even were ZEG attained in the near future we would be faced with major energy supply problems and exacerbation of the present spectrum of environmental insults. It is also unrealistic to expect energy, at the per capita levels of ZEG in the United States, to be available globally. Do we then accept as inevitable a continuation of gross inequality in energy availability between nations?[15]

Energy Conservation Programs and Their Critics

Energy conservation programs have been proposed by others besides the Ford Foundation Energy Policy Project. The Carter administration's energy policy proposal calls for energy conservation and suggests a reduction in energy growth to 2 percent per year. In addition, various so-called public interest groups such as Common Cause, Friends of the Earth, and the Consumer Federation of America have called for energy conservation and endorsed specific measures to attain it.

The National Energy Plan. In April 1977 the Carter administration made public its energy policy proposals under the title *The National Energy Plan*. Although a number of objectives were stressed, the plan's importance for the subject under consideration here is that it stressed conservation and fuel efficiency as the cornerstone of the policy proposals.

Conservation is cheaper than production of new supplies, and is the most effective means for protection of the environment. It can contribute to international stability by moderating the growing pressure on world oil resources. Conservation and improved efficiency can lead to quick results. For example, a significant percentage of poorly insulated homes in the United States could be brought up to strict fuel-efficiency standards in less time than it now takes to design, build and license one nuclear power plant.[16]

The plan goes on to note that although energy conservation means certain sacrifices such as lower automobile horsepower and higher prices for energy-intensive goods, "energy conservation, properly implemented, is fully compatible with economic growth, the development of new industries, and the creation of new jobs for American workers."[17] The choice before the United States is clear, according to the plan: either Americans must reduce the rate of growth of energy consumption, or we must face the possibility of severe curtailments in the 1980s.

The National Energy Plan proposes a number of policies that are aimed at reducing energy use without focusing on particular energy resources. Among the most important are the following:

- a tax on automobiles with low fuel efficiency and rebates on those with high fuel efficiency
- a standby gasoline tax that would be put into effect if consumption exceeded certain annual targets
- tax credits for approved residential and business conservation measures
- requirement that regulated utilities offer complete insulation service to their residential customers
- reform of gas and electric utility rate structures.[18]

Proposed oil and natural gas policy. The most important part of the National Energy Plan is the proposed oil and gas policy. As indicated earlier, oil and gas together account for three-quarters of United States energy consumption, and their price and availability are central to the energy market as a whole.

The major reform proposed in the President's plan is that the price of newly discovered oil would be allowed to rise to the 1977 world oil price level over a three-year period. Oil prices that as of 1977 were controlled at $5.25 and $11.28 per barrel, depending on when the deposit was discovered, would be allowed to rise as fast as the general rate of inflation. The intention of the plan is to encourage more production without letting producers gain windfall profits.

To encourage conservation, the plan proposes a crude oil equalization tax on domestic oil. The tax would be imposed in stages until all domestic oil, regardless of which of the three controlled prices applies to it before taxes, would have a gross price equal to the price of internationally traded oil. The net revenue from this tax would be distributed through tax reductions and payments to the poor.

Reform in natural gas pricing includes moving toward a Btu equivalent price that would link the price of gas to the price of oil, with a small additional amount charged to the industrial and utility sectors. Households would be charged a Btu equivalent price of gas net of the equalization tax. Moreover, the distinction between intrastate and interstate gas would be removed. The stated objective of this policy is to encourage more natural gas development than now occurs and to avoid the distortions that occur with the present system.

Other proposed policies. Through a system of tax incentives and regulations, the Carter administration hopes to reduce the use of oil and natural gas and increase the use of coal in industry and utilities. This policy would be supplemented with environmental regulations aimed at avoiding the undesirable environmental effects of mining and burning coal.

Although the National Energy Plan gives nuclear energy only cautious endorsement as a possible source of a large share of future energy resources, it places greater faith in other sources that until now have not been widely used. "America's hope for long-term economic growth beyond the year 2000 rests in large measure on renewable and essentially inexhaustible sources of energy. The Federal Government should aggressively promote the development of technologies to use these resources."[19]

In summary, it seems fair to say that the National Energy Plan, although it places emphasis on the conservation of oil and gas, expects that under its proposals other sources of energy gradually will be substituted for these two fossil fuels. Thus, while the hope is to "reduce gasoline consumption 10 percent below its current level,"[20] the administration also envisages a yearly increase of total energy demand somewhat below 2 percent. The average annual rate of increase from 1947 to 1976 was 2.8 percent.

The plan's critics. One critic of the National Energy Plan is Walter J. Mead, professor of economics at the University of California, Santa Barbara. "Economists who have specialized in energy economics," he writes, "have argued for greater reliance on market forces and less government interference in energy problems."[21] Carter's plan, in his view, promotes a very different policy and relies on just such government interference. The reliance on government controls is particularly undesirable when associated with what Mead sees as a mistaken emphasis on energy conservation:

The analysis sets out to reduce "energy consumption." This is a myopic view of economic problems. Conservation as an economic problem, requires that *all* resources be "conserved," not just energy. Policies that use tax incentives and the allocation power of government to mandate reduced energy consumption lead, through resource substitution, to higher consumption of *other* resources (copper, insulation, steel, and the like) as if they had no value. This "energy myopia" is an unfortunate and serious economic flaw in the energy plan.[22]

Mead singles out the proposal of continued price controls for oil and natural gas as particularly harmful. The undesirable effects of such controls, he contends, are shortages, a reduction of incentives for oil and gas firms to produce and a consequent rise in imports, and diversion of resources to monitoring the control system that could be better used elsewhere. He also challenges the objection that removing controls would handicap lower-income consumers, since "poor people who do not have a natural gas hookup do not benefit by artificially low prices of natural gas, but owners of large houses with winter gas heat and summer gas air conditioning . . . benefit immensely."[23]

Although Mead is in general critical of the plan, he does believe it contains several praiseworthy suggestions. Specifically, he believes allocative efficiency will be improved if the price of all oil is made equal to the world price, even if it is equalized with a tax. Also, "some of the reforms of public utility rate regulation will lead to greater economic efficiency in that regulated industry."[24]

Another economist who regards the National Energy Plan as fundamentally mistaken in its policy recommendations is Edward Mitchell. Among the observations he makes that are pertinent to the question of reducing energy consumption are:

- Conservation is not generally cheaper than production of new supplies.
- There should be no preference given to the use of resources that exist in greater quantity. We want cheaper resources, not abundant ones.
- The United States is not a "wasteful" nation in its use of energy.
- Energy is not a moral issue.
- Last, and above all, we do not need a comprehensive energy program run in minute detail by the government.[25]

In particular, Mitchell criticizes policies that would establish a different price for oil depending on whether it is used to make gasoline or home heating oil. Similarly, the effects of the proposed policies are such that "if we heat our house with solar energy, the government pays for part of it, but if we heat with oil or gas, we pay our own way." In addition, Mitchell contends that the proposed pricing policy for oil would have the effect of encouraging OPEC to keep its oil prices high. "Under the Carter plan OPEC is given an invitation to raise its price since it has been informed that we will not raise our prices in response."[26]

Mitchell's objections to the plan are in large part also directed at more general issues:

The enthusiasm for conservation as "value" has . . . given rise to a newspeak wherein terms like *efficiency* and *waste* are given new meaning. For example, when the Bureau of Mines released its 1976 energy statistics, it referred to the fall in energy consumption per unit of Gross National Product as "indicating more efficient use of energy per GNP dollar." . . . It is simply impossible to become more "energy efficient" in this sense without becoming less "something-else-efficient" because the GNP by definition has to be spent on something. There is nothing in the study of economics that suggests that there ought to be less energy in the GNP and more ice cream, or anything else. The general supposition is that people ought to use their GNP in the way that pleases them. Pronouncements to the effect that we should not allow energy consumption to grow at a rate of more than 2 percent or 0 percent . . . are expressions of personal sentiments.[27]

Policy Proposals from Other Sources. The Sierra Club has taken an active part in efforts aimed at influencing energy policy, particularly those aspects that have environmental implications. Among the conservation ideas advanced by the club are:

- Change the mandate of various federal government agencies, such as the Tennessee Valley Authority and the Interstate Commerce Commission, "to eliminate energy promotion and require consideration of energy conservation."
- Establish a high-level agency to plan energy conservation.
- Impose a gasoline tax which would start at 10 cents per gallon and increase for several years.
- Institute minimum efficiency standards for automobiles.
- Have the government take over railroad rights-of-way, so that the roadbeds would be maintained by government in the same way that the government maintains highways.[28]

Michael McCloskey, executive director of the Sierra Club, suggests that artificial inducements to economic growth be reduced or eliminated, and that positive constraints be raised to limit energy growth and to protect the environment. He argues:

There has been a basically pro-growth bias in public policy that has been accumulating historically over the course of time that provides a variety of inducements to energy growth. These are embodied in a web of subsidies that run from providing large discounts for industrial consumers of electricity to the Price-Anderson Act to subsidize and encourage nuclear power, to the giveaway of hydropower sites and so on.[29]

In sharp contrast to the views expressed by the Sierra Club and Michael McCloskey are those of Richard Mancke, author of *The Failure of U.S. Energy Policy:*

Even if energy prices rise sharply, the present linkage between levels of energy demand and GNP must remain tight in the short run because of a lack of economic substitutes; however, it will loosen considerably as time passes . . . The time required to complete most of the transition from short run to long run could easily exceed 10 to 15 years . . . United States energy policymakers are charged with the important responsibility of securing supplies of energy sufficient to meet the demands of a growing economy, and at the lowest possible costs. Implicit in this charge is acceptance of the premise that more growth is good. Energy policymakers are not in a position to challenge this premise.[30]

Mancke also argues that past U.S. energy policy, considered as a whole, has been marked by disorganization and conflicting objectives. While some policies, such as tax preferences for the oil industry, encouraged production, others, such as FPC regulation of natural gas and state market-demand prorationing schemes, restricted production.[31]

The Conservation Foundation also has turned its attention to the topic of reducing energy consumption. In a detailed survey of energy use and the possibility for conservation in the United States, the Conservation Foundation concluded, "There exists a variety of practical ways to reduce energy consumption without reducing our material standard of living or demanding significant changes in lifestyles."[32] Among these methods are better home insulation, improved design of commercial and public buildings, recycling certain waste materials, and changing federal and state regulation of gas and electric utilities.

The Conservation Foundation notes, however, that in the long term, even if we succeed in reducing energy consumption now, a positive rate of growth of energy use implies that the United States will again be using at some time in the future as much energy as it does now.

So we see that "energy conservation" is not the ultimate answer to the dilemma of growth vs. quality of life. Unless we redirect many basic institutional, cultural, and economic forces, reducing waste can only serve to *buy time*. But at the rate at which modern technology and social attitudes are capable of change, a grace period of a decade or two might make a great difference.[33]

Another organization that concerns itself with energy issues is the Committee on Economic Development (CED). Its position, although encouraging greater conservation, also argues in favor of increased supplies. Moreover, "energy policy should rely primarily on market incentives in production, distribution, and consumption. Government actions should be a supplement to, not a substitute for, market forces in the allocation of energy resources."[34] The CED also disputes the advisability of setting goals for energy consumption:

It is impossible to predict with certainty the future economic, environmental, political, and technological conditions in which an energy policy must operate. It is equally impossible to predict precisely which new energy programs will work or to set goals with full assurance that they can be met. For this reason, the government should provide for a significant margin of safety in energy planning and should be careful to avoid commitment to a rigid set of policies or targets. What is needed is a flexible approach, involving many different elements of both conservation and production, that can be modified periodically to deal with events as they unfold.[35]

Conclusion

As this chapter shows, several issues implicit in the debate resolution calling for a reduction of energy consumption in the United States are controversial. First, there is argument as to whether the goal of energy conservation (even interpreted as a reduction in energy growth rates) is worthwhile pursuing as a national policy. The dispute here hinges in part on whether businesses and consumers are capable of determining how to use energy efficiently and willing to do so. If they are, it is argued, then measures to promote energy conservation promote the misuse of resources taken as a whole. In part, however, the objection to increased use of energy is philosophical. The use of energy should be decreased, it is said, because of the effect of technical and material advance on human values and the environment. The reduction of energy consumption, in this view, is seen as a way of slowing the rate of economic growth and the use of resources in general. An objection raised to this proposal is that what people want is evidenced by their daily decisions, and these decisions indicate that they are willing to work and pay for the energy they use.

No agreement exists concerning the best means of bringing about energy conservation. The opinion in some quarters is that a reduction of energy use is best achieved by raising the price of energy. Others respond that such a policy would have little effect on energy consumption, or that it would have unfavorable consequences for the poor. It is also argued that simply educating the public on certain matters such as appliance efficiency and economical home insulation will help reduce energy demand. The response is that such a view is naive because it presupposes that consumers stay ignorant for very long about facts that could save them a considerable amount of money.

Although fundamentally different notions about how the economy operates and what constitutes the good life are evident in the discussion concerning each of the debate resolutions, these differences are perhaps clearest in the discussions about reducing energy consumption.

NOTES

[1] Lawrence Rocks and Richard P. Runyon, *The Energy Crisis* (New York: Crown Publishers, 1972), pp. xii, xvi.

[2] Ford Foundation Energy Policy Project, *A Time to Choose: America's Energy Future* (Cambridge, Mass.: Ballinger Publishing Co., 1974), p. 11.

[3] Ibid., p. 46.

[4] Ibid., pp. 46–78.

[5] Ibid., pp. 83–86.

[6] Ibid., pp. 95–96.

[7] Ibid., p. 325.

[8] Ibid., p. 326

[9] Morris A. Adelman and others, *No Time to Confuse*

(San Francisco: Institute for Contemporary Studies, 1975), p. 78. For one man's view of the controversy surrounding the Ford Foundation Energy Policy Project see Lewis Lapham, "The Energy Debacle," *Harper's,* April 1977.

[10] Adelman, *No Time to Confuse,* p. 87.

[11] Ibid., p. 110.

[12] Ibid., p. 13.

[13] Ford Foundation, *A Time to Choose,* p. 163.

[14] Adelman, *No Time to Confuse,* p. 35.

[15] Ford Foundation, *A Time to Choose,* p. 356.

[16] U.S., Executive Office of the President, *The National Energy Plan* (Washington, D.C., 1977), p. x. As of April 1978, a new administration energy proposal was in preparation.

[17] Ibid.

[18] Ibid., p. xv. Natural gas and electric utility rates are generally considered to be set at inappropriate levels. Ernest R. Habicht, Jr., director of the Environmental Defense Fund, has persuasively stated the case against the present structure of electricity rates: "Prevailing regulatory and tax policies lead to prices for electricity that are, with very few exceptions, far below the cost of added power supplies. . . . Electricity users operate with incredibly bad incentives. . . . Most rate structures strongly discourage the conservation of electricity." (Quoted from U.S., Congress, Senate, Subcommittee on Energy and Power, *Hearings on the National Energy Act,* Part III, vol. 1, 95th Cong., 1st sess., May 1977, p. 224.)

[19] Executive Office, *National Energy Plan,* p. xxii.

[20] Ibid., p. xii.

[21] Walter J. Mead, *An Economic Appraisal of President Carter's Energy Program* (Los Angeles: International Institute for Economic Research, 1977), p. 14.

[22] Ibid., pp. 20–26.

[23] Ibid.

[24] Ibid., p. 10.

[25] Edward J. Mitchell, *Energy and Ideology* (Washington, D.C.: American Enterprise Institute, 1977), p. 7.

[26] Ibid.

[27] Ibid., p. 6.

[28] "Sierra Club Conservation Ideas," in Andrew S. McFarland, *Public Interest Lobbies: Decision Making on Energy* (Washington, D.C.: American Enterprise Institute, 1976), pp. 135–136.

[29] U.S., Congress, Senate, Committee on Interior and Insular Affairs, *National Goals Symposium: Hearings on Energy and National Goals,* Part I, 92nd Cong., 2d sess., October 20, 1971, pp. 118, 132.

[30] Richard B. Mancke, *The Failure of U.S. Energy Policy* (New York: Columbia University Press, 1974), pp. 5–6.

[31] Ibid., pp. 143–150.

[32] David B. Large, *Hidden Waste: Potentials for Energy Conservation* (Washington, D.C.: Potentials for Energy Conservation, 1973), p. 4.

[33] Ibid., p. 112.

[34] Committee on Economic Development, Research and Policy Committee, *Key Elements of a National Energy Strategy* (New York, 1977), p. 6.

[35] Ibid., p. 8.

Chapter 5

ENERGY INDEPENDENCE

*Resolved: That the federal government should establish
a comprehensive program to significantly increase the energy
independence of the United States.*

The concern in the United States about the nation's vulnerability to having its oil imports disrupted has led policy makers and observers to consider a number of possible measures for reducing or eliminating those imports. Whether energy independence is a desirable goal, and whether a comprehensive federal program is needed to encourage it, are two points on which no consensus exists however. The third debate resolution calls on the federal government, as defined in the discussion of the first debate proposition in chapter 3, to establish a comprehensive program that would significantly increase the energy independence of the United States. The alternative would be some form of nonactivist federal policy relying on private enterprises and private citizens, as influenced by the market forces of supply and demand, to determine the extent of the country's dependence on foreign energy sources.

By *comprehensive,* the proposition indicates that the program to increase energy independence should deal with all aspects of energy production and consumption that now cause the United States to depend on other countries for energy. Possible *programs* to increase the energy independence of the United States include imposing tariffs or quotas on imported energy sources, providing federal subsidies to domestic production or construction of reserve capacity, subsidizing the development of alternatives to energy imports such as shale oil or synthetic fuels, encouraging reliance on nuclear power and coal, imposing energy taxes to reduce consumption, and imposing mandatory regulations such as minimum fuel efficiency to enforce conservation.

To *increase significantly* the energy independence of the United States would require reducing our reliance on energy imports from foreign countries until the United States is no longer vulnerable to political blackmail or economic disruptions by foreign energy suppliers. To be *energy independent* means not to be susceptible to serious inconvenience from foreign governments' energy export policies, either because energy imports are small or because energy exporters

have no potential for carrying out damaging policies. The proposition does not call for complete independence, only for a significant increase in energy independence.

Klaus Knorr, professor of public and international affairs at the Woodrow Wilson School, Princeton University, asserts:

> the vulnerability of the United States caused by its dependence on foreign supplies for oil, and especially on oil imports from the OPEC countries—and among these, from the Arab members of the oil cartel . . . constitutes a serious risk to the assured availability of energy in the United States; that this vulnerability can be exploited for politically coercive as well as economic purposes, and thus represents a political as well as economic weakness; and that any sensible U.S. energy policy must include provisions for reducing this national vulnerability to acceptable proportions compatible with the economic, political, and military integrity of this country.[1]

Oil is the energy source of primary concern, since in 1977 46 percent of the oil consumed in the United States was imported, whereas this country imports less than 5 percent of its natural gas and is a net exporter of coal.

> According to Douglas R. Bohi and Milton Russell, the long-run well being of the United States may best be served by accepting a reasonable level of dependence on foreign sources, while at the same time creating for the oil-exporting countries a vested interest in facilitating a continuous flow of oil and capital throughout the world.[2]

What constitutes a "reasonable" level of dependence is difficult to quantify and is the subject of much disagreement. Whether the federal government should establish a comprehensive program to increase significantly the energy independence of the United States depends first on whether our current and future reliance on foreign sources involves such a great risk to national security and economic well-being that new federal policies are necessary. Also to be considered are the costs and benefits of introducing policies to promote energy independence, and whether limited intervention in a few critical areas of energy production or consumption would be inferior to a comprehensive program.

Foreign Dependence on Energy since World War II

In 1947 the United States became a net importer of oil, that is, it imported more oil from foreign countries than it sold abroad from domestically produced sources.[3] By 1955 oil imports had quadrupled as a result of rapidly expanding low-cost production in Venezuela, Iran, Iraq, Kuwait, and Saudi Arabia.[4] In the 1950s voluntary import control programs were organized, but new firms entering the oil-importing business raised imports by another 40 percent, threatening the ability of domestic producers to maintain levels of domestic production.[5] In March 1959 the federal government instituted the Mandatory Oil Import Program, imposing a quota fixed as a percentage of domestic production which lasted until 1970. The effect of the quota was to promote the development of domestic production capacity and to maintain domestic crude prices about 60 percent higher than foreign prices. Another result of the quota was that U.S. dependence on foreign imports stayed at less than 25 percent of domestic oil consumption (see table 5-1). The annual cost of this degree of energy independence to consumers was estimated to be around $6 billion because of the rise in cost of oil products in 1969.

In 1967 the Arab countries instituted a boycott against the United Kingdom and West Germany in retaliation for air support they alleged those countries gave to Israel during the Six Day War. The boycott lasted only one month and did not cause serious problems in either country. As the effects of the boycott were limited and the United States was not directly involved, this country was not sufficiently concerned at the time to design new policies to promote our energy independence.

After 1970 the government relaxed oil import quotas in the United States to meet the projected gap between domestic demand and domestic production at prevailing energy prices. Domestic crude prices were frozen in August 1971 as part of President Nixon's general wage and price control program, and they have generally remained under controls since then. As a result of the more liberal quota policy and domestic price controls which tended to discourage domestic production, net petroleum imports in the United States increased from 21 percent of total consumption in 1969 to 28 percent in 1972. In April 1973 President Nixon removed the mandatory quotas entirely and replaced them with a less restrictive system of license fees or tariffs which further

Table 5-1
Crude Petroleum, Petroleum Products, and Liquefied Natural Gas
(millions of barrels)

Year	Consumption	Domestic Production	Imports	Exports	Net Imports[a] as a Percent of Consumption
1960	3,586	2,916	644	74	16
1961	3,641	2,983	700	64	17
1962	3,796	3,049	760	61	18
1963	3,921	3,154	775	76	18
1964	4,034	3,209	827	74	19
1965	4,202	3,290	901	68	20
1966	4,411	3,496	939	72	20
1967	4,584	3,730	926	112	18
1968	4,902	3,883	1,039	84	19
1969	5,160	3,956	1,155	85	21
1970	5,364	4,129	1,248	94	22
1971	5,553	4,078	1,433	82	24
1972	5,990	4,103	1,735	81	28
1973	6,317	4,006	2,283	84	35
1974	6,078	3,832	2,231	80	35
1975	5,958	3,667	2,210	76	36
1976	6,391	3,577	2,676	82	41
1977[b]	6,712	3,636	3,169	83	46

[a]Net imports are imports minus exports.
[b]Preliminary.
Source: U.S., Department of the Interior, Bureau of Mines, *Minerals & Materials*, February 1978, p. 19.

encouraged oil imports. Not only had America's imports expanded greatly in the early 1970s, but between 1967 and 1973 those of Western Europe and Japan combined nearly doubled, indicating the magnitude of the growth of the major industrial states' energy dependence in the early 1970s.[6] Klaus Knorr has described the oil embargo of 1973:

Following the outbreak of the Yom Kippur War in October 1973 between Israel, on the one hand, and Egypt and Syria, OAPEC—that is, the Arab members of OPEC—cut oil production by 25 percent, and placed an embargo on oil exports to the United States. The announced purpose was to compel the industrial importing nations, and in particular the United States, to modify their policies toward the Arab-Israeli conflict in favor of the Arab cause, and to induce Israel to return all Arab territories it had conquered in the earlier 1967 war and kept under occupation since then. This action on the part of the Arab countries was not merely the use of monopoly power for extracting monopoly profits—although that happened, too, as oil prices quadrupled to around $11 per barrel—but also the coercive employment of economic leverage in matters of high diplomacy. . . . With substantial domestic oil production of its own, a great deal of oil in transit on the seas, imports from other oil-exporting countries, and the ability of the oil companies to adapt the pattern of shipments to minimize the impact of the embargo, this country could be inconvenienced but was not very vulnerable.[7]

Not all members of OPEC are Arab nations, and OPEC's non-Arab members, including Venezuela and Iran, continued to export oil to the United States, as did non-

members of OPEC such as Canada.

In 1973 imported oil accounted for about 35 percent of U.S. oil consumption, or about 17 percent of total energy use in this country. "The 1973 embargo caused United States oil imports to fall only from 6.6 million barrels per day in November 1973 to 5.1 millions in January 1974. Thereafter, imports rose to 5.5 million," Klaus Knorr notes.[8] The cutback in energy supplies available to the United States therefore represented only a small proportion of this country's total energy use, but it did cause some economic disruptions. Some schools closed for extended winter vacations, and long lines formed at gasoline stations when price increases were limited by federal price controls.

Japan and Western Europe were much more dependent on energy imports than the United States at that time; oil imports represented 85 and 63 percent respectively of their total energy supplies. They were quick to comply with the Arab demands and issued declarations supporting a United Nations Security Council resolution calling on Israel to withdraw from Arab areas it had held since 1967. The United States, on the other hand, continued supporting Israel, approved additional military aid for Israel, and initiated peace negotiations in the area.

As can be seen from table 5-1, the United States has become even more dependent upon imported oil since 1973; by 1977 net imports had risen to about 46 percent of domestic consumption. In terms of its expenditures on oil, the United States is even more dependent on imports, since domestic oil prices are controlled at levels below world oil prices and the United States must pay the world price for its imports. Table 5-2 shows annual imports of petroleum for the major noncom-

Table 5-2
Annual Imports of Petroleum
(transaction value in billions of dollars)

Year	United States	France	West Germany	Italy	Nether-lands	United Kingdom	Japan	Canada
1960	1.5	0.7	0.7	0.5	0.5	1.4	0.1	0.4
1969	2.6	1.6	2.0	1.6	0.9	2.1	2.3	0.6
1970	2.8	1.9	2.3	1.9	1.3	2.2	2.8	0.6
1971	3.6	2.4	3.2	2.4	1.8	2.9	3.6	0.7
1972	4.6	3.0	3.3	2.6	2.1	2.9	4.5	0.9
1973	8.1	3.9	5.7	3.6	3.0	4.1	6.7	1.2
1974	26.1	10.8	12.5	10.4	5.6	10.6	21.1	3.1
1975	26.6	11.0	11.8	9.3	5.8	9.3	21.0	3.5
1976	34.2	13.3	14.0	10.2	7.3	10.0	23.3	3.5
Percent increase, 1973–1976	322	241	146	183	143	144	248	192

Source: U.S., Department of Commerce, Bureau of International Economic Policy and Research, *International Economic Indicators,* December 1977, p. 62.

munist industrial countries, plus the percentage increase in expenditures on imported oil from 1973 to 1976. Although all countries spend more on oil imports since OPEC quadrupled prices, the increase in expenditures on imported oil in the United States far surpasses those in France, West Germany, Italy, the Netherlands, the United Kingdom, Japan, and Canada. In Knorr's opinion,

> Japan, and especially the West European countries, are at present somewhat less vulnerable than three years ago. Their governments will not panic in the event of another embargo, as they did in 1973. They have appreciably augmented their reserve stocks, and prepared themselves for emergency rationing. They have also kept their energy consumption from increasing at previous rates.[9]

One reason for the increasing foreign dependence in the United States is that American consumers have been sheltered from the full impact of the increases in world oil prices since 1973. Averaging the controlled lower prices of domestic oil with higher imported oil prices (through a complicated series of entitlement payments among refineries) resulted in lower than world prices for consumers. By controlling prices below world prices, the federal government in effect subsidizes consumers and encourages them to purchase more imported oil than they would if domestic prices were not controlled (or if taxes were imposed equal to the difference between the world price and controlled domestic prices, as proposed by the Carter administration in the National Energy Plan). Current federal government policy also promotes dependence on foreign energy sources to the extent that price controls discourage domestic oil production. According to the National Energy Plan, the "increasing consumption of imported oil has led to deepening dependence on the world import market and growing vulnerability to a supply interruption."[10]

Danger of an Oil Embargo

The damages that an oil embargo could inflict on the United States depend, of course, on the number of countries participating, the amount of imports cut off, and the potential petroleum substitutes and alternative sources of energy available. The potential magnitude of such damages should be considered before any attempt is made to determine appropriate policy alternatives. Were all sources of oil imports to the United States cut off, the disruption to the economy would be sizable: it could conceivably reduce national income in the short

run by a multiple of the $45 billion of oil imported in 1977. But the possibility that all the oil-exporting nations in the world would unite to deny oil to the United States is generally regarded as an extremely remote possibility. More likely would be another embargo by the Arab members of OPEC.

Our dependence on oil imported from Arab nations and fear of an oil embargo or future price increases by OPEC may influence the direction of U.S. foreign policy. Oil-rich Arab states could use their greatly increased power and wealth to prod the United States to take a favorable position on a Middle East peace settlement or to induce the United States to increase sales of advanced weapons and aircraft to Arab nations. The extent to which economic concerns do and should be allowed to influence foreign policy positions is controversial and also hard to detect. On controversial issues such as sales of F-15 aircraft to Saudi Arabia and other Middle Eastern countries, some parties fear that American positions may be unduly influenced by our current dependence on oil imports and Arab suppliers. Other parties are concerned that U.S. foreign policy does not adequately reflect the country's best economic interests.

How much harm an embargo could cause is disputed. In 1973 the country the Arabs most frequently classified as an enemy was the United States because they perceived America's strong support for Israel as a significant hindrance to a permanent peace settlement. While it is sometimes argued that the Arab nations could not enforce an embargo of all oil exports for any length of time, James Akins considers even this a straw man. The usual Arab threat, he contends, is not to cut off all oil supplies to all nations, but to supply oil to friends of the Arabs and to deny supplies to their enemies.[11] Morris A. Adelman, professor of economics at M.I.T., disagrees, however:

> The then secretary general of OPEC summed it up very nicely by saying you can't just have a partial boycott or a "selective embargo." The same ground was reploughed by the 1970 report of the Oil Import Task Force. On this point they were unanimous, neither the [American] State Department nor anybody else dissented, when they said that in order to have a security problem you had to have a denial of all Arab oil to all customers.[12]

OPEC is a strong international organization, which Akins doubts will break up from internal friction. But even if it did lose some of its cohesion, a collective Arab embargo is not the only threat. Akins argues that if any one of the seven largest OPEC countries decided to hold its oil off the world market, a temporary but significant world oil shortage would ensue. The loss of production from any two of these seven countries could cause a crisis and "quite possibly a panic among the customers."[13] In the future, however, if the United States imports a significant portion of its oil, and if all the members of OPEC, not just the Arab members, join in the boycott, "the disruptions would be colossal."[14]

Whether all the members of OPEC will join in any future boycott, as Akins implicitly assumes, has been challenged by Adelman:

> If in 1980 we assume that the United States is importing as much as 10 [million] barrels a day and if all Arab oil is cut off, there will be far more than 10 [million] barrels from non-Arab OPEC members to supply the United States. They will divert their shipments from non-American customers to American and they will do this not for love and not for fun, though they will enjoy spiting the Arabs. They'll do it for money. The Arabs will ship more to Europe and Asia so the net result will be simply a big, confusing, costly, annoying switch of customers and no harm otherwise to the United States.[15]

Adelman contends that this is what happened during the 1967 embargo, and that although at that time Germany and the United Kingdom were much more dependent on Mideast oil than the United States will be in 1980, they were not severely distressed by the embargo.

Danger of High and Unstable Oil Prices

Although it is difficult to say how much damage would result from an OPEC embargo, it is clear that OPEC can affect oil prices. For the United States, the importance of the price of world oil is very much linked with *how much* oil is imported (this has not been the case for most of the European countries and Japan, which must import almost *all* their oil). The effect on us of the world price also depends on whether the price of domestic crude oil can be successfully isolated from world oil prices. At present high oil prices are an issue because of the effects they have been having on the Western industrial economies and on developing countries without oil resources of their own. Before 1973 most nations of the world had built up a stock of homes, appliances, factories, automobiles, and other energy-using equipment that were much less energy efficient than is currently optimal at today's higher energy prices. The large jump in energy prices caused a budgetary crunch in many nations in that many factories and other facilities had to be extensively renovated or replaced to improve their energy efficiency. When added to higher fuel bills,

these costs were a large burden on citizens and governments of oil-importing countries. The problems of adjustment caused by the one-time price increase are transitory, though, and by now a large proportion of the adjustments to the new higher level of oil prices have been made.

Since OPEC has significant monopoly power at present and can set oil prices at will, oil-importing nations see a danger that OPEC may use its power in a destabilizing manner. For example, temporary large increases in oil prices followed by large decreases, then increases again, and so on would be injurious to the world as well as the U.S. economy. Highly variable energy prices would raise continuous problems of adjustment as the energy efficiency of the nations' capital stock had to be adjusted continually in response to changing prices. In addition, because the OPEC cartel may be somewhat unstable and because member countries with excess oil-producing capacity have a strong incentive to cheat on the cartel and lower their prices a little to increase sales, there is a possibility that oil prices could fall substantially at any time. This too could be at least temporarily disruptive to countries like the United States that produce part of their own oil supplies. Price cuts by OPEC members could undercut sales by domestic producers and possibly drive some domestic producers out of business, thereby raising domestic unemployment and also making the nation even more vulnerable to any subsequent rise in prices. The present potential instability of oil prices also increases the uncertainty and risks involved in developing alternate domestic sources of energy—such as shale oil, synthetic fuels, or even solar energy—which would not be competitive if oil prices fell.

Domestically, as has already been mentioned, high prices for oil raise quite different issues. In addition to the question of whether domestic oil prices should continue to be controlled or should be allowed to come up to world levels, there are also the questions of how much a rise in crude oil prices would be transmitted to the prices of refined products, and how large the impact of another increase in real oil prices on the economy would be. In the past, doubled and quadrupled crude oil prices have meant increases in the prices of gasoline and heating oil on the order of 10 to 50 percent.

Some economists familiar with the international oil market doubt that OPEC can raise the real price of crude oil much beyond its present level. In fact, at present prices, say these observers, there is evidence of an oil "glut." In early 1978, for example, OPEC's output had to be trimmed from 32.5 million barrels per day to 29 million barrels per day because consumption was down at prevailing prices.[16] The higher the price of oil is set, the greater the incentives for importing countries to develop alternative sources of energy and more efficient ways of using it. This tends to increase the excess oil-producing capacity of the OPEC countries. When combined with the high potential profits of increased sales for any cartel country that independently cut its price while other members maintained theirs, this excess capacity increases the probability that the OPEC cartel will break down. The result would be a drop in crude oil prices, possibly causing major upheavals among domestic energy producers, who depend on rising prices to cover their production costs.

Economic Consequences of Oil Imports

As an M.I.T. study has noted, ''Oil is the largest single item in international trade, and the markets in which this commerce takes place are diverse and complicated.''[17] The tremendous rise in expenditures on oil imports in the United States and other countries has caused great concern about what impact this may have on exchange rates (the rate at which one currency, such as the American dollar, may be converted to another, such as the Japanese yen); on world financial or capital markets; and on oil-importing countries' balance of trade (the divergence between imports and exports). Another fear is that the hundreds of billions of dollars now being paid to OPEC may lead to the disruption of international markets, since countries like Saudi Arabia with relatively small populations are thought to show little desire or willingness to increase their imports of goods and services to match their increased oil revenues.

Table 5-3 compares United States exports to and imports from OPEC and other selected oil-exporting countries during the first and fourth years since the great jump in oil prices. One striking thing about these figures is how much less the United States has been exporting to oil-exporting countries (and OPEC countries in particular) than these countries have been exporting to the United States. In 1974 the discrepancy between U.S. exports and imports was $12.3 billion; by 1977 it had risen to $21.9 billion. This does not necessarily mean that the United States runs an overall balance of trade deficit (in fact, in 1975, it ran a record surplus), since other countries may run trade deficits with the United States. Oil-exporting countries similarly may not run a trade balance surplus if on the whole they import more than they export. Thus, the figures in table 5-3 are insufficient to give a picture of the overall trade balance of any of these countries, or of the seriousness of the problems of a U.S. trade imbalance with the oil-exporting countries.

One immediate result of the oil-exporting countries' huge increase in revenues following the price increases of 1973 and 1974 was that those nations accumulated large reserves of foreign currencies or liquid assets (such as short-term interest-earning debt instruments which may be exchanged for currency in a short period of time). Economists expressed fears that Arab countries would use their reserve holdings to disrupt various countries' foreign exchange markets by switching their holdings from one country to another:

> [The] large accumulation of dollars (and other currencies) in the hands of a small group of countries could be used for political or economic blackmail. The danger to the monetary system could be minimized, however, by cooperation among the major financial centers. If, for example, the oil-exporting nations decided to dump their dollar holdings in international money markets in exchange for Deutschmarks and yen, the potential disruptive effect would be neutralized if German and Japanese monetary authorities chose to accommodate the exchange and add the dollars to their reserves. No exchange rates need be changed; the oil-exporting countries would have simply exchanged their dollars for another currency. If the oil exporters then decided to sell their mark and yen holdings, Germany and Japan could use their newly acquired dollars to purchase them back. Otherwise, an accommodation among the United States, Germany, and Japan could be reached with regard to the outstanding dollars. These transactions require the active participation and cooperation of official central banks; they cannot be handled by private institutions alone.[18]

Although foreign exchange markets may appear to be disorderly to many private citizens and businessmen, most economists believe that they have been functioning in an orderly although perhaps somewhat volatile fashion since the rise in oil prices.

Another issue concerning national security is the potential ability of the Arab nations to purchase strategic American firms or assets with their newly acquired wealth. For a foreign power to control certain key industries or dominate ownership in certain areas of the country would increase the risk of attempted manipulation of or intervention in domestic affairs by foreign countries, which most likely would not be in the national interest. On the other hand, investment in American assets by foreign oil-exporting countries also increases those countries' incentive to act responsibly

Table 5-3
U.S. Trade with OPEC and Selected Oil-Exporting Countries, 1974 and 1977
(millions of dollars)

Country and Area[a]	U.S. Exports[a]		U.S. Imports[a]	
	1974	1977	1974	1977
OPEC and selected oil-exporting countries	8,137	16,476	20,462	38,346
OPEC	6,723	14,019	15,636	33,030
Other than OPEC	1,414	2,456	4,825	5,316
Western hemisphere	2,766	4,634	9,410	8,683
Bahamas	253	224	957	1,050
Leeward and Windward Islands	34	65	27	9
Trinidad and Tobago	192	306	1,272	1,658
Netherlands Antilles	193	304	2,009	1,286
Venezuela[b]	1,768	3,171	4,671	4,072
Ecuador[b]	326	565	473	609
Middle East	3,441	7,953	4,345	12,175
Iraq[b]	285	211	1	382
Iran[b]	1,734	2,731	2,132	2,789
Kuwait[b]	209	548	13	38,215
Saudi Arabia[b]	835	3,575	1,671	6,359
Qatar[b]	34	113	80	292
United Arab Emirates[b]	230	515	366	1,641
Oman	37	57	21	424
Bahrain	80	203	61	74
Asia	553	802	1,697	3,610
Indonesia[b]	531	763	1,688	3,491
Brunei	—	39	—	119
Africa	1,377	3,086	5,010	13,878
Algeria[b]	315	527	1,091	3,065
Tunisia	87	111	22	11
Libya[b]	139	314	1	3,796
Egypt	455	982	70	170
Nigeria[b]	286	958	3,286	6,096
Gabon[b]	33	30	162	225
Angola	62	38	378	310
Congo (Brazzaville)	—	12	—	32
Zaire	—	114	—	173

— Zero or negligible.

[a]Figures do not include port-to-port shipping charges. Totals are sums of unrounded figures and may vary slightly from sums of rounded amounts.

[b]Member of OPEC, the Organization of Petroleum Exporting Countries.

Note: Countries included in this table are: (1) members and associate members of OPEC; (2) less developed countries, 50 percent or more of whose total annual exports (by value) to the United States are petroleum and its products; and (3) less developed countries whose total exports to the United States of petroleum and its products amount to $50 million annually and comprise no less than 25 percent of total U.S. imports from that country.

Source: U.S., Department of Commerce, Bureau of the Census, *Highlights of U.S. Export and Import Trade,* December 1975 and December 1977, table 8.

to safeguard the value of their investments, which might reduce the risk of future disruptive oil embargoes.

The United States ran a trade deficit of $27 billion in 1977, and many have argued that high oil imports are the major cause.[19] In addition, in 1977 and early 1978, the value of the dollar depreciated in terms of several other major countries' currencies, raising the prices of imported goods, and oil imports often have been cited as a major cause of the depreciation. The trade deficit, or excess of imports over exports, has both positive and negative aspects. If other countries are willing to accept and hold American dollars in exchange for their goods and services, then Americans benefit as consumers, since the resource and consumption value of the imported goods exceeds by far the value of the paper on which money is printed and truly represents a major bargain for the country as a whole. Similarly, if other countries are willing to invest in American securities (stocks and bonds), then Americans are able to consume more or build more homes and factories.

President Carter addressed the issue of the impact of importing large amounts of oil on the U.S. economy and national security as follows:

This excessive importing of foreign oil is a tremendous and rapidly increasing drain on our national economy. It hurts every American family.

It causes unemployment. Every $5 billion increase in oil imports costs us 200,000 American jobs. It costs us business investments. Vast amounts of American wealth no longer stay in the United States to build our factories and to give us a better life.

It makes it harder for us to balance our Federal budget and to finance needed programs for our people. It unbalances our nation's trade with other countries. This year, primarily because of oil, our imports will be at least $25 billion more than all the American goods that we sell overseas.

It pushes up international energy prices because excessive importing of oil by the United States makes it easier for our foreign producers to raise their prices. It feeds inflationary pressures in our own country.

Our biggest problem . . . is that we simply use too much—and waste too much—energy. Our imports have more than tripled in the last 10 years. Although all countries could afford to be more efficient, we are the worst offender. Since the great price rise in 1973, the Japanese have cut their oil imports. The Germans, the French, the British, the Italians have all cut their oil imports. Meanwhile, although we have large petroleum supplies of our own and most of them don't, we in the United States have increased our imports of oil more than 40 percent.

. . . The excessive reliance on foreign oil could make the very security of our nation increasingly dependent on uncertain energy supplies. Our national security depends on more than just our armed forces. It also rests on the strength of our economy, on our national will, and on the ability of the United States to carry out our foreign policy as a free and independent nation.[20]

Whether dependence on imported oil actually did contribute heavily to the trade deficit or the depreciation of the dollar is controversial. Some have argued that the trade balance and the level of exchange rates are determined primarily by the desirability of a country's assets to foreigners as investment opportunities, the country's productivity, and the results of monetary and fiscal policies on domestic inflation; any one commodity traded in international markets, including oil, is of minor importance in determining the trade deficit or exchange rates of a large country such as the United States. Although it imported $26.6 billion worth of oil in 1975, the United States ran a record $11 billion trade balance surplus. Japan and West Germany both import large volumes of oil, and although they have little domestic oil of their own, they ran trade surpluses of $10 and $18 billion respectively in 1977. These statistics clearly do not support the contention that oil imports necessarily have a harmful effect on the U.S. trade balance.

Policies to Promote Energy Independence

In November 1973 former President Nixon first initiated Project Independence, a plan aimed at making the United States invulnerable to oil embargoes or price increases by OPEC or other nations. In its original form, the project's goal was complete energy self-sufficiency by 1980. Soon after the initial proposal, this objective was scaled down to significantly increasing the energy independence of the United States. Major studies were undertaken to investigate ways the United States could achieve this goal and reduce its vulnerability to economic disruptions. Increasing our energy independence has continued to receive high priority, and in the Carter administration's National Energy Plan "an immediate objective that will become even more important in the future [is] to reduce dependence on foreign oil and vulnerability to supply interruptions."[21]

Among the possible strategies for increasing U.S. energy independence are accelerating domestic supplies, energy conservation and demand management, and emergency programs.[22] Domestic energy supplies may be increased in several ways, as was noted earlier. Offshore drilling on the continental shelf could be encouraged by modification of federal leasing policies. Accelerating and streamlining environmental impact statements and siting permits for nuclear power plants could speed up new construction by several years. Other environmental regulations, such as those on strip mining or air-polluting emissions, could be relaxed to increase the production and use of coal. The federal government could pass tax subsidies to help producers finance construction of plants or directly subsidize the production of shale oil and synthetic fuels. Eliminating price controls on domestic oil and natural gas would increase incentives to produce more of these traditional domestic energy sources. Direct subsidies and tax incentives could be implemented to promote research, development, demonstration, and installation of new technologies such as solar energy.

But while policies such as these could increase U.S. energy independence substantially, the National Energy Plan cautions that this might not be an unmixed blessing:

A crash program to meet growing demand through increased domestic production would have very serious adverse consequences. Oil, the most critical energy resource, would be drained rapidly, and therefore the nation would not have adequate protection against future shortfalls in energy supply. It would be unwise to solve a problem of short-term vulnerability arising from dependence on oil imports by creating a problem of long-term vulnerability arising from depletion of America's resources.

Finally, an all-out production effort would raise questions of regional equity and balance. Actual and potential producing states would be pressed to deliver increasing quantities of energy at the expense of their environment and, in some areas, a distinctive way of life.[23]

Energy conservation and demand management may take several forms. The government could increase energy prices—especially that of oil—by eliminating domestic price controls, by placing taxes on oil and possibly other energy sources, or by increasing the tariff on oil imports, the aim of such a price increase being to decrease consumption. The regional impact on consumers might vary significantly depending on which method was selected. Quotas on oil imports could be imposed to limit our foreign dependence directly; quotas would probably also result in price increases, which could induce consumers and industry to cut back on energy use. The United States might be able to force the oil-exporting nations to reduce their oil prices by means of a tariff or quota if it has sufficient power as a major purchaser of oil in world markets.

Not all oil-exporting countries are members of OPEC, and among OPEC's members are several countries that are not unfriendly to the United States. Imports from many of these countries form a reasonably secure source of oil supplies. Tariffs or quotas could be imposed against other suppliers who are considered undependable sources or who might participate in another embargo against the United States or its allies. To exclude imports from secure foreign sources as well as insecure ones would unnecessarily raise the cost of energy. Discriminatory import policies might be hard to administer, however, and might violate international rules as established in the General Agreement on Tariffs and Trade (GATT).

Other means of conserving energy include setting new energy efficiency standards for new automobiles, houses, offices, factories, and appliances. Taxes could be imposed on less energy-efficient products and rebated to purchasers of energy-efficient products. New laws or regulations might be passed to induce people to become more energy efficient, such as the national maximum speed limit of 55 miles an hour. The building of new oil or gas plants for generating electricity might be prohibited to help limit the growth in demand for these fuels.

Each of these proposals has its costs and benefits. In the November 1974 summary report on Project Independence, the Federal Energy Administration noted a few of the positive and negative features.

Implementing a conservation strategy has positive environmental effects and alleviates constraint problems, but:

- It requires intervention and regulation in previously free market areas.
- It results in increased nonmarket costs due to more limited individual choice and changed lifestyles.[24]

Emergency programs that might be undertaken to increase the energy independence of the United States include rationing programs and prohibition of "Sunday driving" and other energy-consuming activities deemed of low social value.

Besides curtailing imports or domestic production, the United States could restrict exports of energy resources such as oil, natural gas, coal, and uranium, retaining these resources for domestic uses only. Restrictions of this kind might be viewed as selfish and unjustified by nations less well endowed with energy resources, and thus could harm American foreign relations. (The United States does currently restrict the exportation of oil to other countries.)

Proponents of the third debate proposition might argue that a comprehensive federal program including several of these options is necessary to increase the energy independence of the United States, to lower risks of supply disruption, or to protect the independence of foreign policy decisions and domestic affairs from intervention by other countries. As one report has put it,

Because the marketplace fails to take account of foreign policy concerns, government may, to protect the national interest, take actions that interfere with the price system. Oil production in the United States has a higher value to the nation than production in Libya, for example, because it is more secure. Yet the market fails to reflect this higher value of domestic oil.[25]

It is of course arguable whether unregulated private markets would place proper values on domestic and foreign oil resources; but it is also arguable whether it is possible for the federal government to do a better job of pricing resources. For example, current federal regulations price secure domestic oil resources much lower than the less secure supplies from Libya and other OPEC members. The discrepancies are even more unfavorable in the case of natural gas, where the prices paid for imports are several times the prices paid for domestic natural gas.

Costs of Independence

Either relying more heavily on domestic production of energy resources or reducing energy consumption might involve costs to society—greater domestic pollution, higher costs of energy, dwindling domestic reserves, limited choice among different types of energy, and increased consumption of other scarce resources are all possibilities. Furthermore, significantly increasing the energy independence of the United States means foregoing some benefits of international trade.

If other countries were willing to supply the United States with energy resources such as oil at costs lower than those of domestically produced energy, then America's welfare would be increased even if monopoly profits still were being paid to foreign countries: "When each nation specializes in what it does best and then exchanges with others, we produce more in total and all end up consuming more than if we each tried to be self-sufficient."[26] Countries benefit by being able to trade abundant resources or products they produce relatively cheaply for resources or products that are domestically scarce or expensive. Although the United States depended on imports for 46 percent of its 1977 oil consumption, we are relatively more dependent on imports of bauxite and alumina, chromium, tin, asbestos, flourine, nickel, potassium, gold, zinc, and a number of other minerals.[27] As Douglas R. Bohi and Milton Russell have pointed out,

> The process of international trade and investment necessarily connotes interdependence. Trade in even the most important commodities need not constitute a serious threat to economic security. In fact, petroleum trade, if accompanied (as it must be) by external investment by the most important of the oil-exporting nations, *reduces* the leverage of oil as an economic and political weapon. Oil exporters become increasingly dependent upon the oil consumers.[28]

The United States currently prohibits the exportation of Alaskan oil to foreign countries in order to further its commitment to energy independence and retain domestic supplies for its own use. We benefit from this policy by having abundant supplies and excess capacity available on the West coast. The drawbacks, however, are that the United States is foregoing an opportunity to sell oil to Japan, which currently must import much of its oil from the Middle East. Some of the resources now used to transport oil to Japan from the Middle East could be saved by shipping oil from Alaska to Japan instead, which also could benefit American shippers. Exporting Alaskan crude also would reduce our trade deficit with Japan. Furthermore, as an article in *Business Week* notes:

> If freer oil exports are not permitted, not only will the West Coast crude glut persist . . . but Alaskan producers are not likely to push production. The pipeline flow is now nearing 1.2 million bbl. [barrels] a day and could go to 2 million bbl. fairly easily. Exploration, now slowing up, could produce even more. Furthermore, California wells are being shut in. All this could mean that a bigger market is being created for the Organization of Petroleum Exporting Countries (OPEC), and increasing their price leverage.[29]

Alternatives to Energy Independence

In their book *U.S. Energy Policy: Alternatives for Security,* Douglas R. Bohi and Milton Russell question the ultimate value of programs designed to increase the energy independence of the United States.

> Energy security . . . would assure a continuous supply of energy to consumers at prices that would not fluctuate with each change in the international political situation. The essence of sovereignty is that access to vital goods not be jeopardized by foreign governments. If the contrary situation exists, then foreign policy must forever be hedged by threats to domestic economic vitality. However, while increased domestic output and reduced domestic energy consumption lead in some sense to increased energy security, these policies are very expensive. Moreover, they could also set in motion forces that may tend to support the price of oil in world markets.[30]

There are several forms of insurance the United States might undertake to increase the security of its energy supplies beyond the level provided by private market forces:

> The threat of embargo can be negated by a program of enhanced oil storage. Shut-in capacity would provide the bridge between the short-run response of drawing down oil stocks and the longer-run adjustment of domestic and worldwide supply and demand patterns to changed availability of imported oil.[31]

The federal government could encourage greater storage and stockpiling in the private sector, or it could develop its own stockpiles as is currently being undertaken on the Gulf coast. Also, the government could provide subsidies for excess capacity in the private sector, or drill and cap wells and install the pipelines and equipment necessary to start production at short notice. Because the costs of the resources tied up in idle capacity are high and the temptation to use idle facilities is great, some may not consider this a viable alternative.

Increased national security, dependable energy supplies, enhanced national pride, an improved trade balance, protection against foreign interference or political blackmail in internal or foreign policy matters, and domestic economic stability are all arguments the affirmative side on the debate proposition might use to support its position. A comprehensive federal program, from this point of view, is necessary to assure that U.S. goals of energy independence are achieved. Without such a program, we may continue to depend too heavily on foreign energy sources, since federal policies designed to promote other objectives or the actions of the private sector encourage such dependence. Opponents of the debate proposition might argue that the costs of significantly increased energy independence are too high, that the goal is not worth the loss of the benefits from free trade, that increased federal intervention in domestic and international energy markets would be too costly and complicated to administer, that reliance on private markets to determine the level of energy independence is best, that only limited or narrowly focused federal policies are required, or that the loss of the individual freedoms available in impersonal markets make undesirable a comprehensive program to increase significantly the energy independence of the United States.

NOTES

[1] Klaus Knorr, "Foreign Oil and National Security," in *Oil, Divestiture and National Security,* ed. Frank N. Trager (New York: Crane, Russak & Co., 1977), pp. 106–107.

[2] Douglas R. Bohi and Milton Russell, *U.S. Energy Policy Alternatives for Security* (Baltimore, Md.: Johns Hopkins University Press, 1975), p. 112.

[3] U.S., Executive Office of the President, *The National Energy Plan* (Washington, D.C., 1977), p. 14.

[4] Edward J. Mitchell, *U.S. Energy Policy: A Primer* (Washington, D.C.: American Enterprise Institute, 1974), p. 37.

[5] Ibid.

[6] Knorr, "Foreign Oil," p. 107.

[7] Ibid., pp. 107–108, 111.

[8] Ibid., p. 116

[9] Ibid., p. 114.

[10] Executive Office, *National Energy Plan,* p. 14.

[11] James Akins, "The Oil Crisis: This Time the Wolf Is Here," *Foreign Affairs,* April 1973, p. 465.

[12] Morris A. Adelman, "Is the Oil Shortage Real?" *Foreign Policy,* Winter 1972–1973, p. 73.

[13] Akins, "The Oil Crisis," p. 469.

[14] Ibid., p. 468.

[15] "The Phony Oil Crisis: A Survey," *The Economist,* July 7–13, 1973, p. Survey-24.

[16] "World Oil Glut Brings a Sharper Plunge in OPEC's Production than Anticipated," *Wall Street Journal,* February 22, 1978.

[17] M.I.T. Energy Laboratory Policy Study Group, *Energy Self-Sufficiency: An Economic Evaluation* (Washington, D.C.: American Enterprise Institute, 1974), p. 59.

[18] Bohi and Russell, *U.S. Energy Policy,* p. 9.

[19] "The Reluctant Exporter," *Business Week,* April 10, 1978, p. 54.

[20] "The President's Address on Energy Problems," *Vital Speeches,* December 1, 1977, pp. 98–99.

[21] Executive Office, *National Energy Plan,* p. ix.

[22] U.S., Congress, Senate, Committee on Interior and Insular Affairs, *Project Independence,* 93rd Cong. 2nd sess., November 21, 1974, pp. 57–60.

[23] Executive Office, *National Energy Plan,* pp. 19–20.

[24] Senate, *Project Independence,* p. 63.

[25] Ford Foundation Energy Policy Project, *A Time to Choose: America's Energy Future* (Cambridge, Mass.: Ballinger Publishing Co., 1974), p. 7.

[26] George Leland Bach, *Macroeconomics: Analysis and Applications* (Englewood Cliffs, N.J.: Prentice-Hall, 1977), p. 275.

[27] U.S., Bureau of Mines, Department of Interior, *Min-erals & Materials/A Monthly Survey* (Washington, D.C., February 1978), p. 16.

[28] Bohi and Russell, *U.S. Energy Policy*, pp. 116–117.

[29] "The Case for Permitting Alaskan Oil Exports," *Business Week*, May 1, 1978, p. 48.

[30] Bohi and Russell, *U.S. Energy Policy*, pp. 1–2.

[31] Ibid., p. 12.

Appendix

POSITION STATEMENTS

Short position statements regarding the debate resolutions were solicited from representatives of government and various private organizations. The statements that were submitted are presented here.

Department of Energy

The National Energy Plan articulates ten fundamental principles which form the basic framework of the President's program:

1. Government has responsibility for implementing a national energy policy—informed citizenry must be willing to make sacrifices.
2. Healthy economic growth must continue. Through conservation, our standard of living can be maintained.
3. Environment must be protected through conservation of resources.
4. Vulnerability to potentially devastating embargoes must be eliminated by reducing demand of oil, making the most of our abundant resources such as coal, and developing a strategic petroleum reserve.
5. Sacrifices should be made by consumers and producers of energy alike, thus assuring a fair distribution of responsibility among all walks of American life.
6. The cornerstone of the policy is to reduce demand through conservation.
7. Prices should generally reflect the true replacement cost of energy.
8. Government policies must be predictable and certain.
9. Shifting from oil and natural gas consumption to coal is necessary, taking care to protect the environment.
10. New sources of energy must be developed now.

Next, there are three major objectives of the National Energy Plan spanning three distinct time frames. These time frames are defined as the short term (from now until 1985), the medium term (from 1985 to 2000), and the long term (from 2000 on).

In the short term, the objective is to reduce dependence on foreign oil and to limit supply disruptions by implementing an effective conservation program which would reduce the annual rate of U.S. demand growth to less than 2 percent. The strategies used in this conservation program are: reduce oil imports from a potential level of 16 million barrels a day to less than 6 million barrels; achieve a 10 percent reduction in gasoline consumption; insulate 90 percent of all residences and other buildings; increase coal production on an annual basis by at least 400 million tons; and use solar energy in more than 2.5 million homes.

In the medium term, the objective is to weather the eventual decline in the availability of world oil supplies, caused by capacity limitations, by maximizing the conversion of industries and utilities from natural gas and oil to coal to reduce imports.

In the long term, the objective is to develop renewable and essentially inexhaustible sources of energy for sustained economic growth by implementing a rigorous research and development program to meet U.S. energy needs in the next century.

American Automobile Association

The American Automobile Association shares the belief of many thoughtful and concerned Americans that the U.S. faces a very real and serious energy crisis. The AAA supports the proposition that the near-term solution to this crisis lies in the reduction of this country's growing dependence upon imported oil to meet its energy needs.

At the same time, the AAA maintains a steadfast belief in the ability of the free enterprise system to respond to this situation and solve our energy problems, given the proper incentives, safeguards and competition.

Officials at all levels of government must recognize the importance of the automobile, both as an essential and primary component of our transportation system and as a mainstay of the national economy. This essential role of the automobile necessarily rules out the imposition of harsh restrictions on auto use which would make it extremely difficult for individuals to get to work, to maintain a household and make other essential trips, including recreational trips, necessary to the well-being of the individual and the economic health of the travel industry.

Therefore AAA believes that attempts to deal with energy problems should address directly matters of energy supply, use and conservation. They should not attempt to solve other problems, such as budget deficits, however legitimate those problems may be.

The AAA is opposed to the imposition of taxes or rationing as a means of curbing consumption. Taxes on gasoline at the pump or on crude oil will neither diminish demand nor increase supplies. Gasoline rationing should be avoided, except as a short-term response to a crisis reduction in supply.

AAA strongly urges the development of shale oil which, next to coal, is our largest fossil fuel resource. AAA also urges that additional stationary users of energy be switched from petroleum to other fuels and that steps be taken to increase the availability and use of fuel extenders, such as alcohol, for gasoline.

AAA believes the federal government should do all it can to promote the use of vanpooling, carpooling and charter buses where practical by individuals, communities and large companies. AAA supports voluntary efforts to conserve energy through proper automobile maintenance and improved driving techniques.

American Federation of Labor and Congress of Industrial Organizations

Adequate and secure energy supplies are essential for the United States to provide a healthy growing economy with job opportunities for a growing labor force and a better standard of living and quality of life in future years.

Following is a summary of AFL-CIO proposals in the energy field:

Conservation
- Tax credits for making homes more energy efficient.
- Speedier development of mandatory efficiency standards for new and existing buildings.

- Utility rate reform to eliminate block rates and allow for peak-load pricing.
- Mandatory minimum efficiency standards for major appliances.
- Stronger automobile fleet standards and minimum standards that would not burden moderate-income families.

New Supplies
- Expedite licensing of nuclear reactors by eliminating duplication in reviews by federal and state licensing authorities and streamline federal agency action.
- Expedite policymaking and program development relating to the nuclear fuel cycle, including reprocessing.
- Establish a federal repository for nuclear wastes.
- Expand the nation's uranium enrichment capacity.
- Continue to develop the liquid metal fast breeder reactor program, including the Clinch River facility.
- Continue research into other advanced nuclear technologies, both fusion and fission.
- Develop nuclear export policies that recognize both the need to guard against uncontrolled proliferation of nuclear weapons capability and prospective economic benefits.
- Develop technologies involving solar, geothermal, biomass, shale oil, coal liquefaction and gasification and other potential energy sources.

Energy Authority. Establish a $100 billion federal energy authority to provide direct loans, loan guarantees and other financial assistance to private and public bodies for projects involving both conservation and development of new and additional energy supplies. Federal projects could be patterned on the TVA concept.

Imports. The federal government should take oil importation out of the hands of private industry and deal with oil-exporting countries on a nation-to-nation basis. The government should decide on the amount to be imported, negotiate the price to be paid and provide for allocation. A specific percentage of oil imports should be carried in U.S. flag tankers.

Prices and Taxes. The AFL-CIO opposes efforts to raise the price of crude oil to world prices arbitrarily imposed by the OPEC cartel, as well as efforts to deregulate natural gas prices. Rising prices have had little effect on increasing production or promoting conservation, and benefit only the producers. We also oppose the imposition of a gasoline tax unless such a tax were applied to excess consumption above a basic allotment.

Divestiture. The Congress should break the stranglehold that a few giant oil companies have over the energy industry and the nation by enacting legislation to break up the control they exercise from wellhead to gasoline pump.

Congress should also prohibit ownership of competing energy sources. Oil companies should not also control coal and uranium supplies.

American Gas Association

A maxim of Thomas Jefferson says, ''That government is best which governs least.''

Decades of experience with government regulation at all levels makes gas industry leaders concur with Jefferson. Of course, when a distribution utility has a monopoly for service in an area, it should be subject to regulation. Reasonable local rules aren't an issue. But unreasonable federal controls on gas production and distribution in the United States are a problem, not just for the gas industry but all American energy consumers.

Fossil fuels—oil, coal and natural gas—supply 94 percent of U.S. energy. Of these three forms of hydrocarbon compounds which occur in liquid, solid or gaseous state, only the liquid form, oil, is domestically in short supply. While this shortage requires importation, federal government policy also creates pressure for importing oil because price controls have been maintained on domestic production during the current decade, reducing the incentive to produce. This combination of real and created shortage means we are now importing almost half our oil supply.

The federal government also controls the wellhead price of natural gas sold across state boundaries for consumption in other states. This interstate market has been constricted since 1954; artificially low wellhead prices imposed by the Federal Power Commission (FPC) to benefit consumers have discouraged production. The FPC has been incorporated into the Federal Energy Regulatory Commission (FERC) in the new Department of Energy, but the regulation has continued.

The inevitable consequence of disincentives to production is supply shortage which hits industrial gas users with greatest impact as they are most vulnerable under government priority systems.

Natural gas is the nation's dominant domestically produced energy accounting for 38 percent of all energy developed within the nation. Vast supplies of natural gas remain to be produced domestically. Natural gas will not be depleted before supplemental sources are developed to ensure renewable sources continuously.

The best encouragement for conservation of all forms of energy while stimulating maximum domestic production is to regard the various sources of energy as commodities and let market forces determine their price. United States energy sources should compete on the world market with fuels for import.

If this were the case, U.S. prices would rise, but so would domestic production. And each energy source would compete against others on the basis of its inherent values. Natural gas, which is environmentally benign, would still be the best buy in the nation because of its outstanding system efficiency. Gas comes from the wellhead to consumers through a million-mile pipeline system at 93 percent efficiency.

The fairest system of energy supply lets purchasers decide how much they will pay. It is imprudent to continue allowing the federal government to unreasonably control a commodity so vital as energy.

The American Gas Association and its 300-member transmission and distribution companies have labored intensively, through recent months of debate on formation of a national energy policy, to educate American consumers that they are in the best position to determine prudent use of national resources in free markets. Federal government programs are largely responsible for the status quo, which is a Latin phrase for the mess we are in now.

Jefferson was right.

American Petroleum Institute

Principles. A strong domestic energy industry, consisting of companies both large and small, integrated and unintegrated, operating under competitive market conditions and within existing antitrust laws, will provide the most secure and economical means of supplying the U.S. with energy to maintain economic health, national security, and the welfare of the citizens. Government policy should not preclude potential competitors from investing or operating in any phase of energy exploration, development, production, manufacture, transportation, distribution, or sales.

A practical balance must be achieved between the development of energy resources and protection of the environment. Conflicts between these objectives must be resolved in a timely and efficient manner.

Energy conservation should be encouraged by voluntary means through education and market incentives.

Recommendations. A new direction in federal government policy is needed if the United States is to further its goals of developing domestic energy resources and reducing the degree to which foreign supply interruptions can adversely affect the national economy. This new direction requires that government price controls on oil and gas should be ended since they increase demand and discourage investment in facilities to increase supply. Other counterproductive regulations that restrict oil and gas production and add to its costs should be removed.

Oil and gas exploration and development can best be done by the private sector and not by government. However, federal lands must be made more readily available for oil and gas exploration and development. U.S. jurisdiction over the seabed and subsoil minerals to the outer edge of the continental margin should be retained.

Tax policies which contribute to capital investment, such as accelerated depreciation, investment tax credit, and current deduction of intangible drilling and development costs, should be maintained and improved in order to encourage additional energy related investment.

Research and development on gaseous and liquid fuel technologies should be a private rather than a government undertaking except where incentives are lacking due to extraordinary risks or long lead times, in which case a government role could be appropriate.

Petroleum import policy should continue to allow for foreign supplies adequate to meet national requirements which cannot be met from domestic sources.

National Association of Manufacturers

Accelerated development of domestic energy resources should be the paramount objective of the energy policy of the United States. This acceleration would enhance our strategic national defense, and would help control inflation by making possible greater production of goods and services. It would help avoid the cheapening of the American dollar brought about by enormous balance of payments deficits due to foreign oil purchases. Even the richest country in the world cannot afford indefinitely to import half of its crude oil requirements.

The federal government should not control the development and distribution of energy in the United States other than through existing antitrust laws, but should pursue national policies designed to encourage private enterprise to produce the abundant supplies of energy which this country is capable of producing. This includes oil, gas, and coal production on private, state, and federal lands, both onshore and offshore, and accelerated construction of nuclear, solar, geothermal, and synthetic fuel facilities. Federal control of the wellhead price of natural gas has proved disastrous for the energy economics of the United States by distorting energy markets and investments in energy-producing facilities.

The federal government can best restrain excessive energy consumption by encouraging wise conservation practices and efficient use without regulatory dictation. Information on conservation techniques should be developed and widely disseminated. It should be kept in mind that abundant energy supplies and extensive energy use to displace human labor have a close global correlation with high standards of living and sound, stable governments.

Research and development should be aggressively undertaken to improve the efficiency and flexibility of energy systems; to enhance the supply and use of domestic energy; and to provide future options for harnessing new energy sources. Government policies should encourage research by private industry in commercially oriented matters.

Environmental standards should be realistically modified to recognize that man is a part of the environment and has essential needs which must be reasonably met. Modifications should be directed toward permitting greater reliance on more plentiful domestic resources. Environmental standards must be harmonized to enhance the nation's capability to be self-sufficient in energy.

There is an urgent need to remove statutory and regulatory disincentives to conservation. These deterrents should be identified and remedied.

Since 1972, well before the Arab oil embargo, the National Association of Manufacturers has urged the formulation of a comprehensive, coherent National Energy Policy. The ad hoc, diffuse, and often conflicting approaches to individual energy issues that have marked the past can no longer be tolerated.

There needs to be full recognition that all energy-related matters must be analyzed as parts of a total and unified subject which has as its foundation well-defined energy policy direction, and which recognizes the interplay of economic, reliability, and environmental concerns.

The federal government should establish rational and consistent national policies which will create a long-range economic climate in which producers and consumers can make confident forecasts on which to base long-range plans in an orderly manner. If government does this, then the normal workings of economic supply and demand will have a chance to function so that a crisis from imbalance will not result.

A jumble of punitive tax measures and subsidized tax "incentives" is no substitute for a National Energy Policy.

National LP-Gas Association

What is LP-Gas? The "LP" in LP-gas stands for liquefied petroleum and it simply means that the gas is derived from petroleum products. The term LP-gas refers mainly to propane and butane although propane is by far the predominant type of fuel.

Liquefying the gas provides a highly efficient and safe method of storing and transporting the product. When released from its storage container for use in gas appliances and equipment, one cubic foot of liquid propane will expand to 270 cubic feet of usable gas.

In the United States, about 70 percent of LP-gas is extracted from natural gas and the remaining 30 percent is refined from crude oil.

The LP-Gas Industry. The LP-gas industry is the fourth largest energy industry in the United States. Some 17 million residential, agricultural, commercial, light industrial, and recreational vehicle customers use LP-gas and are referred to by the industry as "traditional and historical users." Approximately 60 million people throughout the country are dependent on LP-gas for one use or another. Most of these customers are located in areas where natural gas is unavailable.

This fuel is undoubtedly one of the nation's most versatile sources of energy. It is available virtually everywhere and because it is portable, an LP-gas system may be installed almost anywhere.

Dependable, clean-burning LP-gas brings city comfort to families in suburban, rural and small town areas. In the home LP-gas is used primarily for cooking, water heating, home heating and air conditioning, and clothes drying. LP-gas is also a staple on farms where it is used for crop drying, poultry brooding, pig farrowing, weed control, tobacco curing, stock tank heating, frost pro-

tection, barn and greenhouse heating. It powers farm tractors, irrigation pumps, trucks, standby generators, and other implements and equipment.

LP-gas has a wide variety of heat and power uses in commercial establishments and light industries. As engine fuel, LP-gas powers industrial lift trucks, buses, taxi cabs, delivery vans, over-the-road trucks, police patrol cars and other vehicles.

The National LP-Gas Association (NLPGA) is a trade association representing LP-gas producers, wholesale and retail marketers, gas appliance and equipment manufacturers, transport firms, tank and cylinder fabricators, appliance, container and equipment distributors and others.

Federal Government Control. LP-gas is under federal price and product allocation regulations which are presently administered by the Department of Energy (DOE). These government regulations control retail prices, maximum profit margins of producers and marketers, and allocation of available supply of LP-gas.

The wellhead price of natural gas going into interstate pipelines is also under federal control. This price control has constricted the petroleum industry's ability to explore and develop new sources of natural gas. Because most propane is extracted from natural gas, the decline in natural gas production has also reduced domestic production of LP-gas from this source.

The NLPGA believes that the deregulation of natural gas and a return to a free market would provide the economic incentive the petroleum industry needs to commit large amounts of capital in the exploration and development of new gas deposits in the United States and in the submerged continental shelf regions on the Atlantic, Pacific and Gulf coasts as well as the waters off Alaska.

This new gas will simultaneously increase the supply of much-needed natural gas for the markets it serves and the supply of propane for its users. Furthermore, a greater supply of natural gas will help prevent diversion of domestic propane to nontraditional users, many of whom are unable to obtain natural gas because of supply shortages. These users can obtain propane from overseas sources with a minimum of government regulation.

Even if natural gas is deregulated, the NLPGA feels that until natural gas supply problems are resolved it is essential to limit simplified propane allocation regulations to the protection of the supply of traditional and historical customers. This would prevent diversion of propane to new high-volume users experiencing curtailment of natural gas supplies.

The NLPGA believes that propane price controls are no longer necessary and should be removed because the domestic supply, combined with the flow of imported propane, is fully adequate for the needs of traditional and historical users.

The Supply of Propane. There is a potential world-wide surplus of LP-gas, particularly in the Middle East where large volumes of natural gas containing propane and butane are being flared off. This waste of valuable natural resources will eventually end because these producing countries are constructing additional natural gas processing facilities to extract the propane and butane, and ship it to markets throughout the world. This will mean more LP-gas available for consumers in the United States.

In 1977 the LP-Gas Industry Advisory Committee to the Department of Energy forecasted that between 1976 and 1980 the total supply of propane available to markets in the United States will increase from 12.9 billion gallons to approximately 16.7 billion, a rise of 29 percent. However, the committee predicted that there will be a dramatic shift in supply sources to more reliance on overseas production while domestic production is expected to decline. Total imports are expected to be 30 percent of total supply by 1980 compared with 7.5 percent in 1976.

Energy Conservation. The NLPGA believes that conservation should be a major element in the nation's energy policy. However, it opposes conservation that is achieved by government-imposed taxes on petroleum and petroleum products which are designed to force prices higher, with the expectation that higher prices will force consumers to conserve. Such a device is inequitable because it creates financial hardship among those least able to afford higher prices for essential fuel and energy.

It is the conviction of the NLPGA that price levels established in a free market will both serve the cause of energy conservation and provide the economic incentive to increase energy supplies. The NLPGA favors a phase-out of price controls on all petroleum products.

National Rural Electric Cooperative Association

The United States recently has experienced a curtailment of its energy supplies of coal, oil and gas due to shortages or supplies, domestic disruptions and international politics. As energy is a completely indispensable ingredient to the operation of our modern society, any impediment to the extraction, conversion and transportation of energy can cause our society irreparable damage. These impediments which appear to directly affect our future energy supply include inadequate fuel reserves, refinery capacity, transportation, equipment and machinery, materials and skilled labor. Indirect impediments such as capital shortages, obsolete federal regulations, monopolistic industrial practices, and irrational environmental regulations can cause equally severe disruptions of our energy supply.

The very future of the electric utility industry is being threatened by the immediate and worsening shortages of fossil fuels, especially oil and natural gas, and the sharp increase in the unit prices of coal, natural gas and oil. These shortages and the resulting price increases threaten the ability of electric utility systems to meet their public responsibility of providing reliable service.

The United States, through the Department of Energy, should establish plans, procedures, laws and regulations which will assure our citizens of an adequate, dependable and reasonably priced supply of energy which is not subject to domestic disruptions or international policies. These plans, procedures, laws and regulations should provide means to eliminate or mitigate all anticipated direct or indirect impediments to our energy supply and should include the following actions or functions:

1. Establish a national energy program which will efficiently and economically consolidate all energy extraction, conversion and transportation functions into an integrated program and which will assure all consumers of an adequate, dependable and reasonably priced supply of energy.

2. Encourage and require the conservation and wise use of energy by consumers through the revision of architectural, automotive and transportation standards and regulations.

3. Thoroughly study the total energy balance in all existing and proposed energy extraction, conversion, and transportation processes to determine that the process itself is efficient and by its introduction does not cause inefficiencies in other processes.

4. Review and revise when necessary federal statutes dealing with all phases of energy extraction, conversion and transportation.

5. Develop contingency plans for cases of catastrophic disruptions of energy supply.

6. Investigate the possible monopolistic practices of industries which control the extraction, conversion and transportation of energy. Particular attention should be devoted to individual companies which produce oil, natural gas, coal and uranium, or who hold substantial interests in reserves of these fuels, or whose boards of directors interlock with those of other energy extraction, conversion or transportation companies and encourage legal action where such investigation warrants.

7. Establish priorities for producing materials, developing resources and training manpower essential to supporting our energy system.

8. Require the preparation of energy impact statements by federal agencies for all major actions which affect the nation's energy supply.

Furthermore, we feel that the federal government should develop and implement a national policy specifically on fuels which should include at least the following elements:

1. Surveillance over the production, marketing and inventory of domestic fuels to avoid price setting by a relatively few large producers.

2. Energy legislation which will provide price incentives for producers in order to stimulate exploration and development of energy reserves in America and will protect the American consumers from exorbitant price increases.

3. Encouragement to business organizations to bring into production new energy sources such as coal, coal gasification, oil shale, geothermal and nuclear, which will result in added competition in the production, processing and marketing of fuels.

4. Vigorous application of antitrust laws to the fuel industries.

5. Establishment of guidelines to maintain a reasonable balance between energy availability and environmental protection.

6. Increased emphasis on research and development of new energy conversion techniques.

7. Coordination and cooperation between energy production and energy consumption industries.

Standard Oil Company (Indiana)

Despite the fact that President Carter has focused attention on the nation's energy problems, very little progress has been made toward establishing a national energy policy that will help us to maintain a more stable energy position.

The obvious solution to many of the most vexing issues regarding energy policy lies in reducing our dependence on foreign energy supplies. That can be done only by increasing our domestic output of energy. To accomplish this, the oil and gas industry must depend on the relaxation of existing price controls, and the orderly, expeditious development of federal onshore and offshore acreage.

In 1977 our country's purchases of foreign oil cost $45 billion and were the major single cause of our balance of payments deficit. If this trend continues, the cost of oil imports may double or triple in 10 years.

Rather than emphasizing domestic energy development, the Carter energy program is based on energy conservation and assumes there is little additional oil and gas remaining to be found in the United States and its offshore waters. The President's conservation-oriented program is to be enforced by taxing domestic crude oil production, and industrial oil and gas consumers failing to convert to coal. There is also a proposed standby tax on gasoline.

The use of this tax money, however, would not be channeled to the oil and gas producers who must finance the crucial exploration and production of domestic resources.

The domestic industry's capital requirements between now and 1985 are upwards of $400 billion. Historically, the industry has been able to generate most of its own funds. Now, because of lost revenues from price controls and rapidly escalating costs, companies must borrow needed capital.

Standard Oil Company (Indiana) proposes a seven-point energy program that would lead to a solution of the country's major energy problems.

1. A pragmatic approach to energy conservation that encourages wise and efficient use of energy but will permit economic growth, provide jobs and still enable citizens to enjoy their accustomed standard of living

2. Prompt removal of price controls on new supplies of domestic crude oil and natural gas

3. Expeditious, yet orderly, development of federal onshore and offshore acreage for production of new supplies of oil and gas

4. Prompt development of the country's vast coal reserves, especially low-sulfur deposits in western states, coupled with a step-by-step program to convert oil- or gas-burning power-generating stations to coal over a five- to ten-year period

5. Establishment of reasonable environmental conditions to permit development of additional energy supplies
6. Intensified research on alternative fuel sources such as coal liquefaction and gasification, solar, and nuclear energy, and oil from shale and tar sands
7. Early action to complete a one-billion-barrel emergency crude oil supply to help protect the nation against another embargo.

BIBLIOGRAPHY

Abbotts, John. *Alternative Energy Scenarios*. Washington, D.C.: Public Interest Research Group, 1975.

Abelson, Philip Hauge, ed. *Energy: Use, Conservation, and Supply*. Washington, D.C.: American Association for the Advancement of Science, 1974.

Abrahamson, Dean E. *Environmental Cost of Electric Power*. New York: Scientists' Institute for Public Information, 1970.

Adelman, Morris A. "Is the Oil Shortage Real?" *Foreign Policy,* Winter 1972–1973, pp. 69–107.

———. "Politics, Economics, and World Oil." *American Economic Review,* May 1974, pp. 58–67.

———. *Security of Eastern Hemisphere Fuel Supply*. Cambridge, Mass.: Department of Economics, Massachusetts Institute of Technology, 1967.

———. *The Supply and Price of Natural Gas*. Oxford: Basil Blackwell, 1962.

———. *The World Petroleum Market*. Baltimore, Md.: Johns Hopkins University Press, 1973.

———, and others. *No Time to Confuse*. San Francisco: Institute for Contemporary Studies, 1975.

Akins, James. "The Oil Crisis." *Foreign Affairs,* April 1973, pp. 462–490.

American Enterprise Institute for Public Policy Research. *United States Interests in the Middle East*. Washington, D.C., 1968.

American Gas Association. *The Natural Gas Supply Problem*. New York, 1971.

American Mining Congress. *The Energy Crisis*. Washington, D.C., 1972.

American Petroleum Institute. *Basic Petroleum Data Book, 1976*. Washington, D.C., 1976.

American Public Power Association, and National Rural Electric Cooperative Association. *Artificial Restraints on Basic Energy Sources*. Washington, D.C., 1971.

Arthur D. Little, Inc. *Energy Policy Issues for the United States During the Seventies*. Arlington, Va.: National Energy Forum, 1971.

Baade, Patricia. *Directory of International Energy Statistics*. Washington, D.C.: International Economic Statistics, 1976.

Bagge, C. E. "Coal: The Once and Future King." *Vital Speeches,* October 15, 1977.

Bartell, T. "Political Orientations and Public Response to the Energy Crisis." *Social Science Quarterly,* September 1976, pp. 430–436.

Ben-Shahar, Haim. *Oil: Prices and Capital*. Lexington, Mass.: Lexington Books, 1976.

Blair, John M. *The Control of Oil*. New York: Pantheon, 1976.

Booz Allen and Hamilton, Inc. *An Inventory of Energy Research*. Washington, D.C.: National Science Foundation, 1971.

Breyer, Stephen G., and Paul W. MacAvoy. *Energy Regulation by the Federal Power Commission*. Washington, D.C.: Brookings Institution, 1974.

———. "The Natural Gas Shortage and the Regulation of Natural Gas Producers." *Harvard Law Review,* April 1973.

Brown, Keith C., ed. *Regulation of the Natural Gas Producing Industry*. Baltimore, Md.: Johns Hopkins University Press, 1972.

Burrows, James C., and Thomas A. Domencich. *An Analysis of the United States Oil Import Quota*. Lexington, Mass.: Lexington Books, 1970.

Cabinet Task Force on Oil Import Control. *The Oil Import Question*. Washington, D.C., 1970.

Chow, Brian G. *The Liquid Metal Fast Breeder Reactor: An Economic Analysis*. Washington, D.C.: American Enterprise Institute, 1975.

Commoner, Barry. "For a New Energy Policy: Toward Using Solar Energy." *Current,* March 1977.

———. *The Poverty of Power: Energy and the Economic Crisis*. New York: Alfred E. Knopf, 1976.

Commoner, Barry, Howard Bokensbaum, and Michael Corr. *Energy and Human Welfare*. New York: Macmillan Co., 1975.

Committee for Economic Development, Research and Policy Committee. *Achieving Energy Independence*. Washington, D.C., 1974.

———. *Nuclear Energy and National Security: A Statement on National Policy*. New York, 1976.

Connery, Robert H., and Robert S. Gilmore, eds. *The National Energy Problem*. Proceedings of the Academy of Political Science, vol. 31, no. 2 (December 1973). New York: The Academy of Political Science, 1974.

Copp, E. Anthony. *Regulating Competition in Oil: Government Intervention in the U.S. Refining Industry, 1948–1975*. Texas A&M University Economic Series, no. 1. College Station, Tex.: Texas A&M University Press, 1976.

Dam, Kenneth W. *Oil Resources: Who Gets What How?* Chicago: University of Chicago Press, 1976.

———. "Implementation of Quotas: The Case of Oil." *The Journal of Law and Economics,* vol. 14, no. 1 (April 1974).

Darmstadter, Joel. *Energy in the World Economy*. Baltimore, Md.: Pub. for Resources for the Future by Johns Hopkins University Press, 1972.

Darmstadter, Joel, J. Dunkerley, and J. Alterman. *How Industrial Societies Use Energy*. Baltimore, Md.: Johns Hopkins University Press, 1977.

DeGolyer and MacNaughton. *Report on National Energy Policy*. Washington, D.C.: Office of Naval Petroleum and Oil Shale Reserves, 1971.

Denton, Jesse C. *An Assessment of the National Energy Problem*. Washington, D.C.: National Science Foundation, 1971.

Duchesneau, Thomas D. *Competition in the U.S. Energy Industry*. Cambridge, Mass.: Ballinger Publishing Co., 1975.

———. *Interfuel Substitutability in the Electric Utility Sector of the U.S. Economy*. Washington, D.C.: Bureau of Economics, U.S. Federal Trade Commission, 1972.

DeCarmoy, Guy. *Energy for Europe: Economic and Political Implications*. Washington, D.C.: American Enterprise Institute, 1977.

Engler, Robert. *The Brotherhood of Oil*. Chicago: University of Chicago Press, 1977.

Enzer, Hermann, and others. *Energy Perspectives*. Washington, D.C.: U.S. Department of the Interior, 1975.

Eppen, Gary, ed. *Energy: The Policy Issues*. Chicago: University of Chicago Press, 1975.

Epple, D. N. *Petroleum Discoveries and Government Policy*. Cambridge, Mass.: Ballinger Publishing Co., 1975.

Erickson, Edward W., and Leonard Waverman, eds. *The Energy Question: An International Failure of Policy*. Toronto: University of Toronto Press, 1974.

Erickson, E., and R. Spann. "Supply Response in a Regulated Industry: The Case of Natural Gas." *The Bell Journal of Economics and Management Science,* vol. 2, no. 1 (Spring 1971).

Fabricart, Neil, and Robert M. Hallmen. *Toward a Rational Power Policy*. New York: George Braziller, 1971.

Fisher, John C. *Energy Crises in Perspective*. New York: John Wiley, 1974.

Foley, Gerald. *The Energy Question*. Hormondsworth, N.Y.: Penguin Books, 1976.

Ford Foundation Energy Policy Project. *Exploring Energy Choices*. Washington, D.C., 1974.

———. *A Time to Choose: America's Energy Future*. Cambridge, Mass.: Ballinger Publishing Co., 1974.

Fraize, W. E., and J. K. Dukowicz. *Transportation Energy and Environmental Issues*. Washington, D.C.: Mitre Corporation, 1972.

Freeman, Roger A. *Tax Loopholes: The Legend and the Reality*. Washington, D.C.: American Enterprise Institute, 1973.

Fried, Edward R., and Charles L. Schultze, eds. *Higher Oil Prices and the World Economy: The Adjustment Problem*. Washington, D.C.: Brookings Institution, 1975.

Gehman, C. "U.S. Energy Supplies and Uses." *Federal Reserve Bulletin,* December 1973, pp. 847–870.

Georgescu-Roegen, Nicholas. *Energy and Economic Myths*. New York: Pergamon Press, 1976.

Gerwig, Robert W. "Natural Gas Production: A Study of Costs of Regulation." *Journal of Law and Economics,* vol. 5 (October 1962).

Glaser, Peter E., and James E. Murphy. *A New View of Solar Energy*. Cambridge, Mass.: Arthur D. Little, 1971.

Gustavson, Marvin. *Dimensions of World Energy*. Washington, D.C.: Mitre Corporation, 1971.

Hagel, John, III. *Alternative Energy Strategies: Constraints and Opportunities*. New York: Praeger, 1976.

Hawkins, Clark A. *The Field Price Regulation of Natural Gas*. Tallahassee: The Florida State University Press, 1970.

———. "Structure of the Natural Gas Producing Industry." *Regulation of the Natural Gas Producing Industry,* ed. Keith Brown. Baltimore, Md.: Johns Hopkins University Press, 1972.

Hoag, Malcolm W. *United States Foreign Policy: Why Not Project Interdependence by Design?* Los

Angeles: International Institute for Economic Research, October 1976.

Hobbie, Barbara. *Oil Company Divestiture and the Press: Economic vs. Journalistic Perceptions.* New York: Praeger, 1977.

Holdren, John P., and Philip Herrera. *Energy: A Crisis in Power.* San Francisco: Sierra Club, 1971.

Hollander, Jack M., ed. *Annual Review of Energy.* Palo Alto: Annual Reviews Inc., vol. 2 (1977).

Houthakker, Hendrik S. *The World Price of Oil: A Medium-Term Analysis.* Washington, D.C.: American Enterprise Institute, 1976.

Illich, Ivan D. *Energy and Equity.* London: Calder and Boyers, 1974.

Institute of Electrical and Electronic Engineers. *The Great Environmental Debate and the Power Industry.* New York, 1970.

Jacoby, Neil H. *Multinational Oil: A Study in Industrial Dynamics.* New York: Macmillan Co., 1974.

Kahn, Alfred E. *The Economics of Regulation: Principles and Institutions* (two vols.). New York: John Wiley, 1970.

Kalter, Robert J., and William A. Vogely, eds. *Energy Supply and Government Policy.* Ithaca, N.Y.: Cornell University Press, 1976.

Khazzoom, J. D. "The FPC Staff's Econometric Model of Natural Gas Supply in the United States." *The Bell Journal of Economics and Management Science,* vol. 2, no. 1 (Spring 1971).

Kitch, Edmund W. "The Shortage of Natural Gas." *Occasional Papers from the Law School,* University of Chicago, February 1, 1972.

———. "Regulation of the Field Market for Natural Gas." *Journal of Law and Economics,* vol. 11 (October 1968).

Kuenne, Robert E., and others. "A Policy to Protect the U.S. Against Oil Embargoes." *Policy Analysis,* Fall 1975.

Laird, Melvin R. "Energy Crisis: Made in USA." *Reader's Digest,* September 1977.

Landsberg, Hans H., and Sam N. Schurr. *Energy in the United States.* New York: Random House, 1968.

Lapp, Ralph E. *A Citizen's Guide to Nuclear Power.* Washington, D.C.: New Republic, 1971.

Lovins, Amory B. "Energy Strategy: The Road Not Taken?" *Foreign Affairs,* April–July 1977.

———. *Soft Energy Paths: Toward a Durable Peace.* Friends of the Earth Energy Papers. Cambridge, Mass.: Ballinger Publishing Co., 1977.

Lund, Leonard, ed. *Energy: Update and Outlook.* New York: The Conference Board, 1975.

MacAvoy, Paul W. *Price Formation in Natural Gas Fields.* New Haven: Yale University Press, 1962.

———. "The Regulation Induced Shortage of Natural Gas." *Journal of Law and Economics,* vol. 14, no. 1 (April 1971), pp. 190–197.

———, ed. *Federal Energy Administration Report of the Presidential Task Force.* Washington, D.C.: American Enterprise Institute, 1977.

MacAvoy, Paul W., and Stephen G. Breyer. *Energy Regulation by the Federal Power Commission.* Washington, D.C.: Brookings Institution, 1974.

MacAvoy, Paul W., and Robert S. Pindyck. "Alternative Regulatory Policies for Dealing with the Natural Gas Shortage." *Bell Journal of Economic and Management Science,* vol. 4, no. 2 (Autumn 1973), pp. 489–492.

———. *The Economics of the Natural Gas Shortage (1960–1980).* Contributions to Economic Analysis 92. New York: American Elsevier, 1975.

———. *Price Controls and the Natural Gas Shortage.* Washington, D.C.: American Enterprise Institute, 1975.

McFarland, Andrew S. *Public Interest Lobbies: Decision Making on Energy.* Washington, D.C.: American Enterprise Institute, 1976.

Macrakis, Michael S. *Energy: Demand, Conservation, and Institutional Problems.* Cambridge, Mass.: M.I.T. Press, 1974.

McDonald, Stephen L. *Petroleum Conservation in the United States: An Economic Analysis.* Baltimore, Md.: Pub. for Resources for the Future by Johns Hopkins University Press, 1971.

Mancke, Richard B. *The Failure of U.S. Energy Policy.* New York: Columbia University Press, 1974.

———. "Petroleum Conspiracy: A Costly Myth." *Public Policy,* vol. 22, no. 1 (Winter 1974).

———. *Performance of the Federal Energy Office.* Washington, D.C.: American Enterprise Institute, 1975.

———. "Oil's Spoils." (Review of Engler, R., *The Brotherhood of Oil* and Blair, J., *The Control of Oil.*) *The Public Interest,* Winter 1978.

Mead, Walter J. *Transporting Natural Gas from the Arctic: The Alternative Systems.* Washington, D.C.: American Enterprise Institute, 1977.

Medvin, Norman. *The Energy Cartel: Who Runs the*

American Oil Industry? New York: Random House, 1974.

Medvin, Norman, Iris J. Lav, and Stanley H. Ruttenberg. *The Energy Cartel: Big Oil vs. the Public Interest.* New York: Association Press, 1975.

Melkus, R. A. "Toward a Rational Future Energy Policy." *Natural Resources Journal,* April 1974, pp. 239–256.

Merklein, Helmut A., and Carey W. Hardy. *Energy Economics.* Houston: Gull Book Division, 1977.

M.I.T. Energy Laboratory Policy Study Group. *Energy Self-Sufficiency: An Economic Evaluation.* Washington, D.C.: American Enterprise Institute, 1974.

Mitre Corporation. *Energy, Resources, and the Environment—Major U.S. Policy Issues.* Washington, D.C., 1971.

Mitchell, Edward J. *U.S. Energy Policy: A Primer.* Washington, D.C.: American Enterprise Institute, 1974.

————. "U.S. Oil Import Policy." *Business Economics,* January 1974.

————, ed. *Dialogue on World Oil: Proceedings of a Conference on World Oil.* Washington, D.C.: American Enterprise Institute, 1974.

————, ed. *Energy: Regional Goals and the National Interest.* Conference Sponsored by the American Enterprise Institute's National Energy Project. Washington, D.C.: American Enterprise Institute, 1976.

————, ed. *Vertical Integration in the Oil Industry.* Washington, D.C.: American Enterprise Institute, 1976.

Mitchell, Edward J., and Peter R. Chaffetz. *Toward Economy in Electric Power.* Washington, D.C.: American Enterprise Institute, 1975.

Mondale, Walter F. "Beyond Detente: Toward International Economic Security." *Foreign Affairs,* October 1974, pp. 1–23.

Moore, W. S., ed. *Horizontal Divestiture.* Highlights of a Conference Sponsored by the American Enterprise Institute. Washington, D.C.: American Enterprise Institute, 1977.

Moorsteen, Richard. "OPEC Can Wait—We Can't." *Foreign Policy,* Spring 1975, pp. 3–11.

Morgenstern, Richard. (Review of Paul W. MacAvoy and Robert S. Pindyck, *The Economics of the Natural Gas Shortage.*) *Journal of Economic Literature,* June 1977.

Mulholland, Joseph P., and Douglas W. Weblink. *Concentration Levels and Trends in the Energy Sector of the U.S. Economy.* Staff Report of the Federal Trade Commission. Washington, D.C., 1974.

Netschert, Bruce C., A. Gerber, and I. Stelzer. *Competition in the Energy Markets.* Washington, D.C.: National Economic Research Associates, 1970.

Nordhaus, W. P. "The Allocation of Energy Resources." *Brookings Papers on Economic Activity, 3.* Washington, D.C.: Brookings Institution, 1973, pp. 529–570.

Novick, David, and others. *A World of Scarcities: Critical Issues in Public Policy.* New York: John Wiley, 1976.

Organization for Economic Cooperation and Development. *Energy Production and Environment.* Washington, D.C., 1977.

Organization for Economic Cooperation and Development. *Energy Statistics, 1974–1976.* Washington, D.C., 1977.

Packer, Arnold. "Living With Oil at $10 Per Barrel." *Challenge,* January/February 1975, pp. 17–25.

Palmer, J. L., J. E. Todd, and H. P. Tuckeman. "The Distributional Impact of Higher Energy Prices: How Should the Federal Government Respond?" *Public Policy,* Fall 1976, pp. 545–568.

Pechman, Joseph A. *Federal Tax Policy* (3rd ed.). Washington, D.C.: Brookings Institution, 1977.

Peabody, Endicott. *Nuclear Energy's Role in Meeting the American Energy Crisis.* Arlington, Americans for Energy Independence, 1975.

Penner, Stanford Solomon, and L. Icerman. *Energy* (3 vols.). Reading, Mass.: Addison-Wesley, 1974–1976.

Phelps, C. E., and T. R. Smith. *Petroleum Regulation: The False Dilemma of Decontrol.* Santa Monica, Calif.: Rand Corporation, 1977.

Resources for the Future. *Energy and the Social Sciences—A Compendium of Research Needs.* Report to the National Science Foundation, October 1973.

Richardson, Harry W. *Economic Aspects of the Energy Crisis.* Lexington, Mass.: Lexington Books, 1975.

Rifai, Taki. *The Pricing of Crude Oil.* New York: Praeger, 1974.

Rocks, Lawrence, and Richard P. Runyon. *The Energy Crisis.* New York: Crown Publishers, 1972.

Ross, I. "Should We Break Up the Oil Companies? Controversy Surrounding Horizontal and Vertical Divestiture." *Reader's Digest,* June 1977.

Russell, Milton. "Producer Regulation for the 1970s." In *Regulation of the Natural Gas Producing Industry,* edited by Keith Brown. Washington, D.C.: Resources for the Future, 1972.

Ruttenberg, Stanley H., and others. *The American Oil Industry, A Failure of Antitrust Policy.* New York: Marine Engineers' Beneficial Association, 1973.

Schantz, Redford L. *Economic Evidence Pertaining to the Supply of and Demand for Natural Gas in the United States with Special Reference to the Permian Basin Producing Area.* Washington, D.C.: Foster Associates, 1971.

Schipper, Lee, and Joel Darmstadter. "The Logic of Energy Conservation." *Technology Review,* January 1978.

Schmandt, Jurgen. *One Aspect of the Energy Crisis: The Unbalanced State of Energy R&D.* Austin, Tex.: Lyndon B. Johnson School of Public Affairs, 1972.

Schnepper, J. A. "Energy Crisis Solution Shining a New Light on the Problem." *Intellect,* December 1977.

Schurr, Sam H., ed. *Energy, Economic Growth, and the Environment.* Baltimore, Md.: Pub. for Resources for the Future by Johns Hopkins University Press, 1972.

Schurr, Sam H., and others. *Middle Eastern Oil and the Western World: Prospects and Problems.* New York: American Elsevier, 1971.

Starratt, Patricia. *The Natural Gas Shortage and the Congress.* Washington, D.C.: American Enterprise Institute, 1975.

Stucker, James P. "The Distributional Implications of a Tax on Gasoline." *Policy Analysis,* Spring 1977.

Sunder, Shyam. *Oil Industry Profits.* Washington, D.C.: American Enterprise Institute, 1977.

Teller, Edward. *Energy: A Plan for Action.* New York: Commission on Critical Choices for Americans, 1975.

Tilton, John E. *U.S. Energy R&D Policy.* Washington, D.C.: Resources for the Future, 1974.

Udall, Stewart, Charles Conconi, and David Osterhout. *The Energy Balloon.* New York: McGraw-Hill, 1974.

U.S. Congress, Congressional Budget Office. *President Carter's Energy Proposal: A Perspective.* Staff Working Paper. Washington, D.C., 1977.

U.S. Central Intelligence Agency. *International Oil Developments.* Washington, D.C., 1976.

U.S. Department of the Interior. *U.S. Energy: A Summary Review.* Washington, D.C., 1972.

U.S. Executive Office of the President. *The National Energy Plan.* Washington, D.C., 1977.

U.S. Federal Energy Administration. *1976 National Energy Outlook.* Washington, D.C., 1976.

U.S. Federal Energy Administration. *Project Independence, A Summary.* Washington, D.C., 1974.

U.S. Federal Energy Administration, Office of Conservation and Environment. *Energy Conservation Study: Report to Congress.* Washington, D.C., 1974.

U.S. Federal Energy Administration, Office of Economic Impact. *Petroleum Market Shares.* Washington, D.C., 1975.

U.S. Federal Trade Commission. *Staff Report on Its Investigation of the Petroleum Industry.* Washington, D.C., July 1973.

U.S. General Accounting Office. *Energy Issues Facing the 95th Congress.* Washington, D.C., 1977.

U.S. General Accounting Office. *G.A.O. Energy Digest.* Washington, D.C., 1978.

U.S. Treasury. "Report on Results of the FTC's Petroleum Investigation." *Daily Report for Executives.* September 7, 1973.

Weidenbaum, Murray L. *Business, Government, and the Public.* Englewood Cliffs, N.J.: Prentice-Hall, 1977.

White, David C. *Summary of Energy Studies and Problems.* Cambridge, Mass.: M.I.T. Press, 1971.

Wildhorn, S. *How to Save Gasoline: Public Policy Alternative for the Automobile.* Cambridge, Mass.: Ballinger Publishing Co., 1976.

Wilson, Mitchell. *Energy.* New York: Time, Inc., 1967.

Yager, Joseph A., and Eleanor E. Steinberg. *Energy and U.S. Foreign Policy.* Cambridge, Mass.: Ballinger Publishing Co., 1975.